the JOY of Giving

– The Paul & Jane Meyer Story

Dr. William M. "Bill" Hinson

The Joy of Giving

— The Paul and Jane Meyer Story

© 2009, by Dr. William M. "Bill" Hinson
10618 Big Canoe
Jasper, GA 30143
wmh@tds.net

Published by The Leading Edge Publishing Company
PO Box 7411
Waco, TX 76714
Ph: 254-776-9001
Fx: 254-751-0475
www.theleadingedgepublishing.com

ISBN 10: 0-89811-509-4
ISBN 13: 978-0-89811-509-3

Printed in the United States of America

RELIGION / Christian Life / Stewardship & Giving

Contents

Dedication. 4

Introduction 5

Chapter #1 The Beginning of Stewardship 9

Chapter #2 It's All God's by Right of Creation 23

Chapter #3 What Stewards Do. 31

Chapter #4 Benefits of Giving 41

Chapter #5 Multiply Your Efforts 49

Chapter #6 Make No Excuses. 61

Chapter #7 Stewardship of Yourself 69

Chapter #8 Stewardship Toward God. 81

Chapter #9 The Mission of Paul & Jane Meyer 89

Chapter #10 Perpetual Stewardship 103

Chapter #11 How Will You Be Remembered? 113

   APPENDIX A: Charitable Giving Annuities 120
   APPENDIX B: Creating a Trust 122
   APPENDIX C: Forming a Foundation. 123
   APPENDIX D: Resources 125
   About the Author 127

Dedication

This book is dedicated to my wife, Bettye, and Paul and Jane Meyer.

The dual dedication is because of Bettye's positive influence on my personal quest to be a faithful steward, and it was easy for me to recognize the faithful blend that Jane has given to Paul in their remarkable lives of stewardship.

Bettye has inspired depth in my sermons, money in my pocket, and a happy Christian home for over 57 years with our children and grandchildren.

Paul and Jane have graciously shared their personal files with copies of letters for the details of this book. Our friendship of over 50 years has given me a special vantage point to give you *The Joy of Giving — The Paul and Jane Meyer Story.*

Dr. William M. "Bill" Hinson

Introduction

This book is about an extraordinary couple, Paul and Jane Meyer.

As a Christian minister, I have performed many marriage ceremonies over the past 59 years. My pastoral goal in pre-marital counseling, writing marriage ceremonies, and participating in the total wedding celebration, always has been based on Biblical principles for husband and wife.

My challenge to husband and wife centered on Ephesians 5 "giving and forgiving" in their sacred relationship is based on God's plan for a successful and productive family.

I have often contemplated where all of these brides and grooms are today as I have not been able to keep up with many of them, but Paul and Jane are the exception. I had the privilege to perform their wedding ceremony, and I have been fortunate to evaluate their marriage from the vantage point of friendship over the years. Their strong and successful marriage relationship has been based on personal and corporate "giving and forgiving."

It has always been a "team response" by Paul and Jane that reveals the joy of giving.

In this book I want to introduce you in a detailed way to the fact that you can experience the joy of giving with this remarkable couple. I recognize that one book does not do justice and cannot encompass all that Paul and Jane do with their time, talent, and treasure.

In the area of stewardship:

- One Texas governor said that Paul and Jane have been instrumental, both directly and indirectly, in influencing more funding to assist the economically disadvantaged to attend college (over 6,000 kids thus far) than any other couple in America.

- They give to many women's causes such as domestic violence, Christian Women's Job Corps, single women in trouble, and more.

- They support and provide funds for buildings and other things to do with the extremely poor and disadvantaged.

- They funded the training of over 1,200 leaders in Third World countries who, in turn, have trained an average of over 100 each to present the gospel national to national in 184 countries in the world.

- They have started several foundations and have encouraged others to start scores of other foundations.

- They have funded development directors' kick-off salaries in numerous major ministries across America.

- Hundreds of pastors in churches of many denominations have used Paul's Christian writings in their sermon preparations.

- Paul and Jane's mission statement is a take-off of John Wesley:

To do all the good we can
In all the ways we can
For all the people we can
In all the places that we can
For as long as we can.

- Their first prayer each morning begins with: "This is the day the Lord has made, let us rejoice and be glad in it," followed by, "Please, Lord, give us someone to minister to and help today."

As a young pastor, I first met Paul Meyer over 50 years ago. He helped me start a church under a tree, and that church is now Wayside Baptist in Miami, Florida. Paul headed up the fundraising efforts and did an incredible job.

I have used all of his leadership courses that he has authored since 1960 in my ministry for myself and my staff at four different churches that I have pastored, plus as Assistant to the President of Baylor University.

I had the great honor for a few years of assisting Paul and Jane with their ministry through the Paul and Jane Meyer Family Foundation. I have taken what I have learned from our relationship into my various positions that I have had over the past 15 years with the Haggai Institute.

Needless to say, I have gained tremendously by being associated with Paul and Jane. That is why I have been trying to get them to let me write this book for the last 25 years. They have said "no" again and again, but I was finally able to convince them to permit me because their inspiring story and example and insights could influence others to reconsider their thinking, belief, faith, and action concerning stewardship.

They are the only married couple I have met in my lifetime of ministry who set a goal to die broke — to give it all away because they know at the get-go that it's all God's by right of creation. I've heard Paul and Jane say many times:

> **"You thought it was fun making it. Well, you don't know what fun it is until you start giving it away."**

> **"We feel guilty because we feel so hilariously happy today and explosive with joy!"**

> **"We may have less because we gave it away, but we gained much more in return, so much so that we don't think it was a fair trade."**

These words come from the hearts of stewards. They can be trusted.

Dr. William M. "Bill" Hinson

"Give bountifully — without thought of getting anything for yourself in return."

— Catherine Bramwell-Booth

CHAPTER 1

The Beginning of Stewardship

"Whatever you vividly imagine, ardently desire, sincerely believe, and enthusiastically act upon must inevitably come to pass."

Paul J. Meyer, an achiever to the highest degree, penned these words many years ago, and for more than five decades, he and his companies have been inspiring millions of people around the world to become winners and leaders in every facet of their lives.

Considered one of the most influential people in the history of the personal development industry, Paul J. Meyer is the No. 1 selling author of personal development material in the world, having sold more than $3 billion worth of materials translated into 24 languages in more than 60 countries. Just a single program, *The Dynamics of Personal Motivation*, has recorded more than $700 million in sales.

Besides these staggering accomplishments, Paul has also started and operates, along with his family, over 40 successful businesses in a multitude of industries, earning him and his family millions of dollars a year.

Over the years, these companies have included: aircraft leasing and sales, airport fixed base operations, auto racing, business seminars, commercial real estate, consumer financing, educational software, equipment leasing, exotic game, fiberglass products, finance, nutrition products, international trade, legal insurance, leadership courses, management consulting, personnel evaluation, printing, personal development and self-improvement courses, residential real estate, time management systems, vinyl products, and more.

This is only a part of his story. Paul is also a devoted husband to his wife, Jane, and they have five children and 15 grandchildren with whom they are very close.

But maybe the most significant thing about Paul is that he is a giver on a grand scale. The foundation that he and Jane started, called The Paul and Jane Meyer Family Foundation, has given tens of millions of dollars in the last 25 years to charities and organizations devoted to making a difference.

Their foundation is only one of more than 55 ministries and charities that Paul and Jane have either started or support with their time, talent, and treasure.

In fact, stewardship is at the core of who Paul and Jane are as people. This passion for giving is legendary and remains the driving force of their lives. Not a day goes by that Paul and Jane aren't making a difference in the lives of the disadvantaged and needy.

Having attained so many accomplishments in every area of life you could be led to believe that Paul Meyer was a product of money and privilege, of connections and silver-spoon opportunities, but nothing could be further from the truth.

Coming to America

In 1920 Paul's father, August Carl Hesse, born in 1891 in Germany, left his native land on a ship bound for America. He was lost at sea for 56 days! However, having worked many years as a furniture maker and craftsman, and saving diligently to afford his fare, hardship was no stranger to August Hesse.

After the initial rough turn of events, he felt his faith renew, his heart fill with courage, and his face break out in a smile when he finally spotted Ellis Island. His dream had come true; he was landing in America! Soon he not only adopted America as *his* country, but he also adopted the last name of his sponsor, a man named *Meyer*.

Paul remembers his dad's pride in America, his unfailing patriotic spirit. "On July 4th my dad always displayed the flag. I will never forget when I was about six, and we were standing at a parade watching the flag go by. My father put his hand on my head and said, 'Paulie boy, always love that flag, and your country, and the freedom the flag represents. Always remember that there was a heavy price paid for it.'"

In fact, Paul's dad entered one of the first floats in the Rose Bowl Parade in 1930. At that time anyone could enter a float, and his dad entered a 1929 Chevrolet truck loaded with flowers … and American flags!

During Paul's youth the family went to every single parade in Campbell and San Jose, California. "We always stood every time they sang "The Star-Spangled Banner" or when they said the Pledge of Allegiance. My father always cried when our nation's flag went by."

There were some hard times with Paul's dad too. He was a tough man in many ways. He was a man who demanded discipline and perseverance from his children; a man who was unrelenting in his expectations; a man who never accepted excuses.

On the 116th anniversary of his dad's birthday Paul Meyer wrote a tribute to his dad, which said in part:

> The Leader of Our Clan was talented and strong
> He worked hard with his hands all the day long
> A master craftsman with wood and with steel
> He taught us to work with an "iron will!"

He showed us, told us, taught us, trained us…
Again, and again, and again

He led us…let us…helped us attain
Without his direction our lives might have been
Mediocre…Dull…Aimless…Vain

The Leader of Our Clan always taught us to "be strong,"
That life can be tough, but we must move on
I wouldn't take for those learning days, for the good and the bad
Or for all the lessons I learned as a lad
I owe so much to him, my devoted and caring Dad.

The Leader of Our Clan has long since passed away
But his blood runs through me at work and at play
He always said, **"Where there's a will there's a way"**
And I always remember what he said each day!

I love him still, this man of steel
The rough times I've forgotten (forgiven)
I remember him for the good he taught
What I learned was not for naught
I learned "I CAN" if I use MY skill
If I take control with an iron will
If I don't look back, but only ahead
I remember these things I learned from my Dad.

A woman's example

August Carl Meyer worked in the shipyards of Brooklyn, New York, for a time and then again in South Carolina. Eventually, at the age of 35 and still single, he moved to California where he was invited to dinner one evening and met his future wife, Isabelle Rutherford. Not being a man to waste time, he proposed just three weeks later!

The concept of stewardship began to take root in young Paul Meyer from watching his mother. He was greatly influenced by his mother's gifts of love, selfless giving, and Christian service. Isabelle Meyer taught Paul through word and deed how to forgive, how to communicate, and how to love God.

Paul remembers his mother pounding into his head to "do the right thing because it's the right thing to do" and to honor his word as his bond; to be dependable, accountable, reliable and credible. "I was taught that you should say what you mean and mean what you say, and that whether you said it or put it in writing, you could be trusted to do what you agreed to do."

Paul recalls a visit from his mother when he was climbing the success ladder in his 20s. "My mother came to see me and saw my home, my car, and other material possessions. She looked me in the eye and said, 'Paul, I am frightened by your early success. Don't forget who gave you the talent, don't forget who owns it all, and don't let Satan use your success to take you away from what's important.' I will never forget her words. I strive to honor her by sharing the abundance that God has given me, Jane, and my family."

In 1969, at age 79, Paul's mother fell in her home and wasn't found for two days (she died a few days later in the hospital with Paul holding her hand). In the apron she was wearing the day she fell, Paul found a note that read: "S.S. HOPE: 7 miles, 7 cents."

He cried uncontrollably, realizing that she had raised 7 cents after walking 7 miles for *S.S. HOPE*, a hospital ship that provided medical care to people in developing nations.

Paul later shared with me, "Her example was the most powerful act of stewardship I have ever witnessed!"

LETTER OF THANKS

Mr. Meyer,

How could I ever say enough. Thank you seems so small, but with my whole heart, God bless you for helping old ladies like me.

The sewage was backing up in my tub and it was not a healthy situation for me. I live alone and on $550 a month and I could not afford to get it fixed.

Thank you for helping me get the sewer line fixed. It is wonderful. Please keep helping people like me that can't afford to get their houses fixed.

Bessie S.

Beginning the vision

Growing up in California during the Great Depression did influence Paul, but it was his parents that made a lasting impression on his attitude on life and work. At the age of six, he was picking fruit with other migrant farm workers. When the foreman complained that Paul was too young to be working, Paul's father said, "Well, we want him to *learn* to work."

Young Paul got it from both ends. One extremely hot day, while working in the grape vineyard and returning home with a bloody nose, he asked his mother, "How long do I have to do this kind of work?" She replied, **"Until you develop the gifts that God gave you." She cradled his head and said, "This is a magic carpet. When you develop it, it will take you anywhere you want to go, and you can be anything you want to be**."

From that moment on Paul made up his mind that people and words were going to be his pursuit. The next day while working in a grape vineyard, the young boy made a pivotal decision. "I prayed and asked Jesus Christ to come into my life. That day He became my Savior and Lord. I wanted to follow Him and develop the talents and abilities He gave to me and that has been my lifelong pursuit."

Sharing with others

As a boy, Paul's family was never financially well off. However, during World War II, they sent some of what they did have to relatives in war-torn Europe. Every few weeks Paul helped his dad box up and send small cartons of dried fruit, jams, nuts, and anything else they could think of that might ease their family's suffering.

"Over 50 years later, after tracking down some of my parent's ancestors in France and Germany," Paul recalls, "I found myself at the home of the very family we had mailed the packages to years before. As we chatted, the discussion turned to World War II, and I asked my cousin if they ever received the boxes my father and I had sent."

His eyes brimmed with tears and his voice cracked as he explained, "We survived because of what you mailed to us. We would not have made it otherwise."

Paul told me later, "My level of trust for my dad went up several notches that day. All the work and effort was instantly worth it."

Developing perseverance

Paul has many stories about his dad's way of teaching him perseverance and discipline, but one event particularly sticks in his mind. When Paul was a boy, he desperately wanted a bicycle, but his dad refused simply to go buy one. He took Paul to a local junkyard where they selected several old bicycles. When they got home, Paul's dad showed him how to strip the bike down to its basic frame. Then his dad said, "Put it back together and you'll have a bicycle."

Sure enough, when all the parts were reassembled, Paul had a whole bicycle! By doing it twice, as his dad insisted, Paul found himself with a business opportunity, and as a teenager he refurbished and sold over 300 bicycles!

Paul explains, "My father showed me that the power of choice is not bound by the money we did or didn't have. That power was mine, and he showed me how to harness it. He helped me unlock the potential that I did not see in myself."

Learning to plan ahead

Paul also grasped the importance of saving early on. "When I was six years old my father drove me to the end of Shelley Avenue off White Creek Road and let me out of the car to pick prunes with migrant farm workers. I picked one lug-box during the day and earned a nickel. I probably still have it."

When Paul was 12 years old, he set out to break the world record. He got up at 2 a.m., hung flashlights in the trees, and worked till late in the evening. "I was wrung out," he says with a smile, "but I made 25 cents a box, or $25.25, which was approximately the same amount that men earned per week at that time."

That night with $25.25 in his pocket, Paul was excited. He went home and was confronted with a lesson he never forgot.

Paul explains, "I was higher than a kite. I told my dad about it. He was reading the paper. He pulled the paper down, looked me in the eye, and said, 'Don't tell me how much you earned today. Show me how much of it you have five years from now, and I'll tell you how much you earned today.'"

Paul has never forgotten that lesson!

Jane learns stewardship at an early age

Jane also learned about stewardship as a young child by being the "recipient" of stewardship. The youngest of four children, she lived on a farm in Central Texas, and at the age of two her father was killed in a tractor accident.

Jane's mother sold the farm and moved into town with three daughters. The oldest child, a son, was serving on the *Enterprise* aircraft carrier during the war.

The family was blessed with great neighbors who reached out to assist the young widow and her three children.

- One neighbor kept a cow and chickens and always furnished fresh milk, butter, and eggs to the family.

- Another neighbor had a garden so the family could always have a supply of vegetables.

- There was even a neighborhood grocery store, and Jane's mother was allowed to purchase groceries on "time."

- Jane also recalls the grocer putting "extra things" in the bag from time to time.

The most important thing to Jane was the neighborhood church they attended. Many of the couples would open their houses to Jane and the other youth. They were always encouraging, supportive, and sharing. Jane was encouraged to do mission work through the church, and this enriched her life by teaching her to reach out to others.

Another important aspect of being involved in the church was that the men became "father figures" to Jane and her sisters, who never knew their father. These godly men spent their time working with the youth of the church, teaching, training, and leading.

Jane's mother had an unbelievable faith that God would provide what the family needed, and somehow help always came through the stewardship of caring friends, neighbors, and relatives.

Jane has always looked back on her childhood, not as a hardship, but rather as a blessing to have been raised totally conditioned to understand at every level the importance of stewardship and to have a steward's heart and attitude.

It was not only Jane's idea to start their foundation, but she also wrote the mission statement.

Positive influences for stewardship

Over the years, there have been many different positive influences on both Paul and Jane for stewardship. Here, in Paul's own words is a brief snapshot of the key people who have influenced Paul and Jane throughout the years:

> **Isabelle Rutherford Meyer:** When I was young, between the ages of six and ten, my family lived in a garage. It was during the Great Depression and we lived out in the country. Basically, everyone in our neighborhood was very poor. There was a creek about a quarter of a mile from our house. It had lots of trees, and lots of hobos stayed out there. The hobos would come by our house and, although we had very little food, my mother would always share some with them. The last week of her life, my mother walked seven miles and raised seven cents for the *City of Hope*, a ministry ship. So, growing up and into my adulthood, I saw stewardship in action!

> **Dr. W. M. "Bill" Hinson:** I started my business career selling life insurance and was very blessed with the results. Because of my mother's example, and because I was also a Christian, I didn't have to think twice about tithing. Dr. Bill

Hinson was my first pastor. He put the right emphasis on stewardship in his preaching.

Robert G. LeTourneau: When I was 24, Bill Hinson took me to hear R.G. LeTourneau speak. LeTourneau was famous for building huge road equipment and offshore drilling rigs. He was about 65 or 70 years old at that time. When I heard him thank God that he could KEEP 10%, meaning that he GAVE 90% of his income, I was over-whelmed! That experience changed my life!

Rev. Billy Graham: Soon after meeting R.G. LeTourneau, I met Rev. Billy Graham at a leadership conference attended by 40 businessmen. At the conclusion of his talk, Rev. Graham said, "Does anyone have any questions?" I said, "Yes, I have one. Why was my pastor called to preach and I wasn't?" He asked me what I did for a living. I said, "I am in the insurance business." He suggested that I consider my business to be my full-time ministry as a Christian steward. That encounter changed my life even more!

Abraham Vereide: Shortly after meeting Rev. Graham, I met the Methodist evangelist Abraham Vereide, whose great hope was to preach the word of Jesus to political and business leaders throughout the world. Vereide believed that the best way to change the hearts and minds of powerful leaders was through discreet personal ministry. Over his lifetime he succeeded to a remarkable degree. The Presidential Prayer Breakfast (now called the National Prayer Breakfast), started by Vereide, has become a tradition in our nation's capital. I was attending one of these prayer breakfasts and Vereide put his hand on my shoulder and said, "God is going to use you in a mighty way as a steward." His comment made an even further impact on my life because of my great respect for him.

Lee Boswell: Then God led me to meet Lee Boswell in Lakeland, Florida. Lee was my No. 1 insurance client and a chief center of influence for my business. All five of his daughters married preachers. He lived very humbly. It was a long time before I knew his real financial wealth and how much of it was dedicated to the Lord and His ministries and charities. Lee was the first example in my life of a wealthy person who was totally sold out to the Lord and who had committed all of his businesses and resources to God's work. I wanted to do the same.

Bernard and Audre Rapoport: The first couple who influenced us to become givers here in Waco was Bernard and Audre Rapoport. They were very committed and dedicated in their support of educational causes, the economically-disadvantaged, and many organizations that improve the lives of residents of Central Texas.

Paul and Katy Piper: The couple that we chose to emulate and follow as Christian stewards was Paul and Katy Piper. Even the name of their foundation, CIOS (Christ Is Our Salvation), told us who they were. We were overwhelmed when we saw the huge sums of money they gave to education, and we set a goal, that if we prospered, we would do likewise. We have now helped thousands attend college through the Passport to Success program. Paul and Katy were the first to introduce us to Mission Waco and all of its ministries. Their influence is behind our gift to provide the Meyer Center for Urban Ministries. At least 25% of what our family foundation gives, comes from the example set by Paul and Katy Piper.

Jane and I thank God that He put all of these people in our lives. It is our hope and prayer that everything they have taught us will continue through our children and grandchildren … the message that it's all God's by right of Creation.

Paul and Jane were deeply affected by these people, and they took action. I love that about them. Consider this quote, one of Paul's favorites, and let it challenge you as you begin your journey of stewardship:

"I shall pass through this world but once. Therefore any good that I can do or any kindness I can show to any human being, let me do it now and not defer it, for I shall not pass this way again."

"The Lord gives to us that we may give to others."

— *Sanford T. Whitman*

============== **CHAPTER 2** ==============

It's All God's By Right of Creation

In less than 100 years, someone else will own what you own today. No one can hold onto anything forever ... an inch of land, a square foot of a house, or a diamond on a ring. Everything will have changed hands — *someone else will own it all!*

Paul and Jane Meyer are very clear about the concept of what belongs to them and what belongs to God. If you ask them why they give, they will tell you simply: "It's *all* God's by right of creation."

They believe that stewardship is the explicit acknowledgement that your financial resources belong to God and that you only manage them on God's behalf.

Some have called stewardship the process of "watching over others' assets." In that sense parents are stewards of their children, teachers of their students, employers of employees, and our government of the proper use of our tax money.

In short, everyone, in one way or another, is a steward.

Many years ago, some tax laws changed, and it affected Paul's real estate investments in a big way. I watched what Paul did. He said to his accountants, "Look, we are entrepreneurs. We have to accept personal responsibility for what happened and deal with it."

Paul had already committed to give a certain amount to several charities. Some of the creditors were not happy with him, but he insisted on paying his charitable obligations first … and he wasn't late on his other obligations either.

I believe that in order to fulfill God's call in our lives, we must first accept the position that we are stewards. We cannot honor God or fully achieve any goal when we believe we are the owners.

Stewardship is really a lifestyle, not just what you do with your money. It starts with your heart, moves to your pocketbook, and then into your entire life. I have personally watched Paul live this out.

There are eternal principles that affect your life, and then in turn affect the lives of others. Let's examine the principles or master keys that Paul and Jane Meyer have credited for their remarkable success:

#1 — God is the Creator and supreme giver

Everything is God's. He made it. It's His. This fact determines how you operate in every area, from how you manage your finances, use your talents and abilities, and even decide the time you spend with your children. In every area of life, this truth has everlasting effects.

Scripture states, *"The earth is the Lord's, and everything in it, the world, and all who live in it"* (Psalms 24:1). God's written word contains every truth that Christians hold dear. In the area of stewardship, Scripture offers much that directly guides us, benefits us, and blesses us.

Since everything is His it helps to keep everything in perspective by remembering the following:

- In a short few decades, none of us will be alive.

- When we're dead we certainly won't own anything!
- If we don't own anything, then we are merely stewards!
- If we are stewards, shouldn't we be the best stewards possible?

We are to live as stewards, not die as stewards.

LETTER OF THANKS

Dear Mr. Meyer,

When I heard that your foundation would pay for the labor and materials to raise my sunken living room floor so my husband with multiple sclerosis could get from one room to the other, I was speechless.

I could not imagine how to adequately express appreciation to someone who so generously gives unselfishly when he sees the needs of others.

Thank you so much from the depths of my heart for your kindness and assistance at a time in our life when it was so needed.

Thank you so very much!
Joan A.

#2 — God is the sustainer of all things

Since He created it all, it is God's job to sustain His creation. He gave us life and since we are part of His creation He will sustain us as well.

Our job is to be obedient and to accomplish His will; it is not to worry about doing the sustaining ourselves.

Scripture states, *"And my God will supply all your needs according to His riches in glory in Christ Jesus"* (Philippians 4:19). When we feel it is our job alone to manage our needs we become over-whelmed and burdened. We will draw back from God's call upon our life because we are unable to see how we can accomplish the enormous tasks that He may ask of us.

> If a person gets his attitude toward money straight, it will help straighten out almost every other area in his life.
> — Billy Graham

God always calls us to something larger than ourselves. He desires that we depend on Him. Only when we realize that God is faithful to supply all we need to fulfill His will can we operate with confidence and peace.

God is always eager to show up and show off on our behalf!

#3 — God is the One who enables us to accomplish far more than we could ask or imagine

Everything we accomplish is the result of Him. Scripture says, *"And you shall remember the Lord your God, for it is He that gives you the power to get wealth, that He may establish His covenant, which He swore to your fathers, as it is to this day"* (Deuteronomy 8:18). While work is still required of us, He is the one who takes what we have and turns it into what He wants it to become.

Consider the boy who gave his meager lunch to Jesus and the 12 disciples. Jesus took the loaves and fish and fed thousands of people!

Jesus still does that today with the gifts and talents we have, but He first requires that we give Him what we have. His desire is to *multiply* it and to positively affect thousands, even millions, of people.

Since all we have comes from God, the concept that "possessions are bad" is both irreverent and irrelevant! If we shun what He gives us or would have us manage, we are not accomplishing His will on earth, which is the goal of every Christian.

Possessions are not a right/wrong issue; they are instead an owner/manager issue!

In addition, a vital link exists between how Christians use earthly possessions and the eternal rewards that Christians receive. The Bible often calls the result of good stewardship the "fruit" that Christians will receive in heaven.

That is God's heart!

LETTER OF THANKS

The Paul and Jane Meyer Family Foundation has been a valuable collaborator with our Meals On Wheels program for many years. The funds we have received over the years have helped feed countless numbers of homebound older adults.

More than half of the total number of meals served is provided through local funds. We appreciate the support offered to our agency by your foundation.

Our Meals On Wheels program offers older, homebound adults a way to deal with lack of funds for food, inability to prepare meals, and the isolation of loneliness.

Sincerely,
Melody McDermitt
Central Texas Senior Ministry

#4 — God is a God of abundance

The good news is that God has more than enough. There is no shortage of supply of anything, at any time, in any area with Him. It is only our thinking and training that limits us or sets the parameters within which we operate.

God wants us to soar as eagles, not fly along the ground like swallows. He wants to propel us like a rocket toward our dreams, not have us settle for the long walk to fulfillment. He wants us to build bridges across raging rivers instead of trying to swim across them. But, we must desire His mindset and work according to God's parameters.

When we act as good managers of God's provision, He is free to entrust us with more possessions to accomplish His will. The issue is never who has more possessions, but rather, what we are doing with the possessions He has entrusted to us.

A great example of this principle is the story of the three servants in the New Testament (Matthew 25) who were each entrusted with a certain amount of gold. Two of them *multiplied* what they had *and were given more as a result*. This makes total sense because God is a steward Himself and invests back into those who are faithful.

What happened to the third servant? He did nothing with what he had been given and so *even that was taken from him*.

We cannot forget that God has a purpose behind the possessions with which He entrusts us. He gives in order that we might build up His kingdom. Everything God gives has a purpose!

#5 — God is a God of grace

If God were not a God of grace, none of us would be here. And the very grace we have is a gift from Him. He gave us everything we have, including eternal life through His son, Jesus Christ. For both reasons, our giving reflects our gratitude.

History reveals that the Jews whose lives were saved by the hand of Oskar Schindler during the Holocaust of World War II showed their gratitude years later by giving Schindler one day's pay per year. Collectively they provided for the man who saved their lives.

Though absolutely fitting and appropriate, Christians understand that Jesus saved them through His death on the Cross. As a result, the fact that they owe Him EVERYTHING is an understatement!

#6 — God calls us to teach others

All stewards play a very important role in the training of others. Teaching the importance of being a steward is an integral part of our walk with God.

Because every area of our life is affected by our actions as stewards, the relevancy and importance of this training only increases with time.

You've heard it said that giving someone a fish is good for a day, but teaching that person to fish is good for a lifetime. Similarly, stewards understand the long-term benefits of educating others about consistent stewardship. It is to be a way of life.

Statistics (according to Giving USA) reveal that on average, Americans give less than 3% of their income to charities per year. *If we consistently gave a full 10% which is only the tithe, there would be enough money to feed, clothe, and house every hungry person on the planet!*

Talk about making an impact! **Teaching others to give is one of the very top priorities of Paul and Jane Meyer.**

"God has given me time, initiative and energy. It's important to use these gifts to help others."

— Sister Ann Catherine Veierstahler

===== **CHAPTER 3** =====

What Stewards Do

Of the many important stewardship qualities, there are certain foundational pillars that bring strength, wealth, balance, and permanence to individuals who recognize their role is that of a steward.

In short, there are certain things that stewards do. I have watched Paul and Jane for many years, and they simply do what stewards do.

#1 — Stewards pay God first with the tithe

Paul is always quick to point out that giving is the only issue in the Bible on which God challenges the believer to put Him to the test. God *dares* a Christian to give. Two of Paul and Jane Meyer's favorite Scriptures on money and stewardship are:

> *"Bring all the tithes into the storehouse, that there may be food in my house, and prove me now in this ... if I will not open for you the windows of heaven and pour out for you such blessing that there will not be room enough to receive it"* (Malachi 3:10).

> *"Give, and it will be given to you; good measure, pressed down, shaken together, and running over will be put into your bosom. For with the same*

> **measure that you use, it will be measured back to you"** (Luke 6:38).

God throws down the gauntlet! He instructs us to test Him at His Word. He asks us to put ourselves and everything we have directly into His hands.

Tithing (giving 10%) is an integral part of stewardship because it accomplishes three important primary objectives:

- **It tells who is Lord of your life** — *"You cannot serve both God and money"* (Matthew 6:24).

- **It requires you to walk by faith** — *"For without faith it is impossible to please God"* (Hebrews 11:6).

- **It allows God to bless you** — *"Then your barns will be filled to overflowing, and your vats will brim over with new wine"* (Proverbs 3:10).

Paul relates the story of being proud of starting to tithe at 27 years of age, thinking that his 10% to God was pretty impressive. Around that time, I invited him to a speech by businessman and philanthropist Robert G. LeTourneau.

What Paul heard floored him! *LeTourneau gave away 90% of his income and lived on the remaining 10%!*

Paul remembers his reaction. "I thought I was right on the verge of being a generous person and I thought, 'If I had 10% left, I would be living in a tent.'"

Paul decided right then and there that he would learn to give more and rely on God more.

He explains, "Giving does something for me that nothing else could do. *In a lifetime, I would simply say the more I have poured out, the more I have had to pour out; and the more I give, the more I have to give.* And I am not just talking about blessing in the form of financial return."

Scripture states, *"Honor the Lord with your possessions, and with the first fruits of all your increase, so that your barns will be filled with plenty, and your vats will overflow with new wine"* (Proverbs 3:9-10). And the more Paul gave, the more God gave in return!

You'll notice that Scripture does not say anything about bringing the tithe "when you can afford it" or paying it "with whatever is left over." Paying the tithe is simply a *principle of stewardship*, whether you have a lot of money or not.

LETTER OF THANKS

Paul and Jane,

Oh my God, what would my 5 kids and I have done this month without you both.

My sincere thanks to you for helping me pay my rent. I had an eviction notice. Thank you, thank you, thank God for all of you.

I lost my job and have not gotten another placement yet and I had no money to pay rent this month.

God needs people like you to help people that have situations financially beyond their control.

Thank you very much,
The McKee Family

Paul actually refuses to counsel those who ask for financial advice but aren't paying their tithe. He simply says, "If you aren't tithing, then my counsel will do you no good. You are to pay your tithe first, then your taxes and bills."

He points out, "We need to get God on our side by showing that we have faith in Him and regardless of our financial mess, we pay Him first and then begin to live on what is left. This is real stewardship faith in action."

#2 — Stewards keep commitments even when it hurts

When Paul lost 90% of his income with the failure of the life insurance company he worked for in the late 1950s, I watched Paul continue to tithe. Did God immediately pour out more blessings than he could contain? *No, things actually went from bad to worse!*

But before long, things began to change, doors began to open, and fresh visions began to come. What Paul ended up with both geographically and professionally could only have come from God!

When we are obedient to God's command, we discover that God *always* keeps His promises.

Paul Meyer's firm grasp of stewardship underlies his entire business style. He fiercely maintains the priority of giving even during periodic business decline and heavy debt repayments.

Faith drives him on when reasonable caution might hold another man back. He and Jane have this positively as their top financial priority.

Your commitment — like Paul and Jane — should be to honor pledges you have made by trusting that God will supply the means to pay them. Ultimately, you must internalize the truth that God will supply:

> *"Be anxious for nothing, but in everything in prayer and supplication with thanksgiving, let your requests be made known to God; and the peace of God, which surpasses all understanding, will*

guard your hearts and minds through Christ Jesus" (Philippians 4:6-7).

#3 — Stewards are financially responsible

Each of us is financially responsible for what we do have control over. This means at the very least that God expects interest on what He gives us.

The servant who buried his master's talent of gold instead of investing it was told, ***"You should have put my money on deposit with the bankers, so that when I returned I would have received it back with interest"*** (Matthew 25:27).

Paul's strong belief is that God desires, for our sake and His, that we *multiply* whatever it is He entrusts to us. Does that mean Paul never made a mistake? Of course not! As he readily admits, "I've lost money in investments and had numerous businesses close their doors." But that doesn't make him a bad steward.

It's the winning over the long haul that matters; which means setbacks are never the end of the road.

#4 — Stewards give nonstop

A giver will always give, regardless of how much or how little he or she might have because *giving is at its core an attitude of the heart.*

Paul and Jane Meyer are the best examples of this of anyone I've seen as a pastor and leader.

Charlie "Tremendous" Jones said it perfectly, **"You can't really enjoy anything without sharing it, and this includes your faith, love, talents, and money. Someday you'll discover we never really give; we are only returning and sharing a small portion of what we have received."**

And no matter how much we give, God will never allow us to give Him more than He gives back. *Never!*

LETTER OF THANKS

Mr. Paul Meyer,

I work as the Program Coordinator at Mission Waco. Although I have never met you personally, I am more than aware of your generous contributions to Mission Waco and other organizations in the area.

I am responsible for all of the benevolence assistance that is done here, so I have the privilege of working directly with the low income and homeless folks in Waco and the surrounding counties.

Without your contributions, we would not be able to provide the assistance that we are currently providing, and I would not have a job. Therefore, on behalf of all those you have touched, thank you from the bottom of my heart.

**Bo Wallace
Mission Waco**

#5 — Stewards use all that they have

People who complain or wish they had what other people have *are not being good stewards over what God has entrusted to them.* Most of the time God gives seemingly small opportunities; then we take it from there.

John Cook, a long-time friend and business associate of Paul's, was diagnosed with polio soon after his first child was born. The doctors said he would be on an iron lung for the rest of his life, but he and his wife believed otherwise. Within no time he was off the machine, and within two years he was 90% restored! Paul hired John as his first employee when he launched his major company, Success Motivation Institute in 1960.

John understood he had to make the best of what life presented. He refused to give up, quit, or be defeated, and he was an inspiration to everyone he met. He could take the seemingly impossible and turn it into something great! Such is the mentality of a steward.

> If you are really thankful, you will share.
> — W. Clement Stone

Paul and I both spoke at John Cook's funeral. I read John's favorite Scripture, Isaiah 41:10. I then quoted John as he had told me on several occasions, "Without Paul Meyer's encouragement to me, I would have been dead 40 years ago."

#6 — Stewards train others as stewards

Stewards *multiply* themselves by training other people to be good stewards. This is especially effective with children. Howard Dayton, CEO of Crown Financial Ministries, says that children need training in four distinct areas:

- Routine responsibilities
- Exposure to work
- Earning extra money at home
- Working with other people

Paul and Jane taught their children early on the concept of tithing, giving, saving, and investing. What they did with their advice and training was up to them, but Paul and Jane are happy to say that all of their children have made wise investments for their families here on earth and for their futures in heaven. And they, in turn, have taught their children the same principles of stewardship.

#7 — Stewards obey and trust God

Stewardship is often condensed into *time*, *talent*, and *treasure*, but Paul believes there is one more ingredient: his testimony.

Being a good steward has everything to do with our relationship with Jesus Christ. Whether we trust Him and obey Him will be answered by the way we handle our finances, and in Paul and Jane's case, the answer is a resounding YES!

As stewards, it is our responsibility to do what God says to do. The outcome is therefore His responsibility.

The rich young ruler in the Bible who went away sad when Jesus asked him to give away his wealth failed to understand that his obedience and trust toward God were all he had to offer: *The wealth he "owned" was already God's!*

> One man gives freely, yet grows all the richer; another withholds what he should give, and only suffers want.
> — Proverbs 11:24

Our hearts determine our priorities, *"For where your treasure is, there your heart will be also"* (Matthew 6:21). Just look at your checkbook for the last 90 days and see where you have placed your treasure!

Patrick Morley, author, businessman, and president of the Man in the Mirror ministry, has dealt with wealthy businessmen for decades. His condensed insight is this: "The greater proportion of a man's income he gives, the happier he is."

Simply put, Paul and Jane do what stewards do.

And so can you.

"Riches without charity are worth nothing. They are a blessing only to him who makes them a blessing to others."

— *Henry Fielding*

CHAPTER 4

Benefits of Giving

Giving is clearly a joy because of the good that comes as a result. It is the act of giving that excites people. It is a blessing to the giver and the receiver.

Here are some of the benefits that Paul and Jane have received from giving:

Giving benefits others!

A few years ago, they received the following letter:

> *It's graduation time! I cannot thank you enough for the scholarship you provided! The money enabled me to earn a Master of Science Degree in Special Education at my own pace, while I began to recover from Rheumatoid Arthritis and a number of other ailments.*
>
> *I remember the day that I read your* Unlocking Your Legacy *book and hurried into the kitchen to tell my mother, "I think the author may be able to help me!" I had no idea how I was going to pay for school; I needed to stay a full-time student in order to be covered under my father's medical insurance. I was disabled and could no longer take out*

another loan "in good faith," and my parents did not have the money to pay for school; however, they really did not have the money to pay for doctor visits with no insurance helping out. You and God came through for me when I needed the help the most.

I cannot thank you enough for reading my letter and deciding to pay for my graduate degree! I will never forget the amazement on my father's face when I told him that you would be financing my graduate degree. I respect your philosophy of giving people a "hand up" and not a hand out so that they will be able to take care of themselves for years to come.

Three years ago I was basically dying, and now I have a Master's degree and I am slowly regaining my health. Thank you so much for taking the financial pressure off of me and allowing me to have a second chance at a career and a better life. Without your help, I would not be the person I am today. Thank you so much for everything you have done for me and for countless others!

— Kacey Long

This letter of thanks, one of a countless number in Paul and Jane's files, witnesses to the simple everyday generosity that marks their lifestyle.

Paul and Jane enjoy giving to others because of the obvious benefits.

A few years ago, Paul was driving home through a neighborhood when he saw a woman trying to push a man in a wheelchair out the front steps of their home. Paul went about 50 more feet and stopped his car. "Who else is going to do something about this?" he asked himself.

He backed up his car and got out, then walked over to the couple. They explained how the man had been confined to a wheelchair just the day before and that they were trying to cope with the new changes. Paul said, "Would you mind if I had a carpenter come and build you a wheelchair ramp?"

They were certainly open to it! And since then, over 200 wheelchair ramps have been put in all across the county, free of charge, thanks to Paul and Jane's generosity.

> Giving is true loving.
> — Charles Haddon
> Spurgeon

The practical need proved to be so large that Paul and Jane started a ministry called **Carpenter's Hammer** within their foundation to not only build ramps but also to outfit bathrooms, among other projects, for senior citizens and those who are handicapped.

Giving benefits you!

When you give, you benefit. Here is a short list of benefits that you enjoy as a result of giving:

- It's essential for a full life.
- It provides joy.
- It brings fulfillment.
- It produces excitement.
- It is rewarding.
- And it's fun!

Consider this advice from Stephen Post, Ph.D., from his book, *Why Good Things Happen to Good People*:

> You wish to be happy? Loved? Safe? Secure? You want to turn to others in tough times and count on them? You want the warmth of true connection? You'd like to walk into the world each day knowing that this is a place of benevolence and hope? Then I have one answer: give. Give daily, in

small ways, and you will be happier. Give, and you will be healthier. Give, and you will even live longer.

How is that for benefits from giving!

Dr. Post goes on to list several more direct, clinically-proven, benefits from giving. These include:

- Giving in high school predicts good physical and mental health all the way into late adulthood, a time interval of over 50 years.
- Giving reduces mortality significantly in later life, even when you start late.
- Giving reduces adolescent depression and suicide risk.
- Giving is more powerful than receiving in its ability to reduce mortality.
- Giving to others helps us forgive ourselves for our mistakes, which is key to a sense of well-being.
- Helping friends, relatives, and neighbors, along with providing emotional support to a spouse, reduces mortality, although receiving the same kind of help does not.
- Even the simple act of praying for others reduces the harmful effects of health difficulties in old age for those doing the praying.

Without question, giving benefits you … and it's a joy!

Giving bounces back!

John Edmund Haggai, founder of the Haggai Institute, once checked in with a business party at the Bali Hyatt on the island of Bali in Indonesia. The hotel manager recognized him and said, "Dr. Haggai, welcome."

John thought for moment, then he remembered the manager from when he last saw him: a teenager hustling bags at the old Intercontinental Hotel in Singapore.

The manager said, "I told my staff that you are our guest. We have assigned you a complimentary suite, the finest in the hotel."

Then he turned to all the people in John's party and said, "This man treated me as well as he treated the head of the corporation when he used to come to Singapore. I could never do enough for him."

LETTER OF THANKS

Mr. and Mrs. Meyer,

I want to express my sincere appreciation for the generous grant you provided for the purchase of a new van for the House Where Jesus Shines Ministry. We were able to locate a 2008 model with only about 5,000 miles on it, which was $6,000 less than the new vehicle.

This van will help us transport men who are ex-offenders to their jobs as they are transitioning back into society. Since God created each of us to be productive, we believe that a man's identity and self-worth is often connected with his ability to work and contribute to his own future.

Thank you for partnering with us to see men restored to God's purpose: as sons, brothers, fathers, and grandfathers.

Sincerely,
Pastor Ronnie Holmes
House Where Jesus Shines

The Bible tells us: *"Whatever a man sows, that he will also reap"* (I Corinthians 6:9).

Writer and philosopher Ralph Waldo Emerson once wrote in an essay titled "Compensation" that the world is so constructed that every action you perform bounces back to you like a ball. **Borrow money, and you incur a debt. Venture nothing, gain nothing. Live honorably, and you will be honored. Love and others will love you.**

While Emerson might tie up the loose ends rather too neatly, still we can see what he's driving at. Giving has a way of bouncing back to you.

Giving lasts a very long time!

Giving has a way of having an immediate effect, then producing many, sometimes smaller, effects down the line. You could say it's like a stone skipping across a pond, except that the stone keeps on skipping, making one strike after another.

These benefits could affect people you've never met, in languages you don't speak, and even decades after you are gone. It's truly an amazing thing to see.

For example, on a visit to the People's Republic of China in 1984, John Edmund Haggai and his wife, Christine, were at a luncheon party in the Shanghai Hotel. As they stepped into the top-floor restaurant, Christine fell and injured her wrist. Fortunately, the party included a doctor, and after making a quick examination, he said, "Let's get her downstairs. My hospital is just across the road."

They crossed the busy street and entered the hospital compound, thankful that advanced medical facilities were located so close by. Only on the way out of the medical compound did they notice a plaque outside the hospital's largest building.

It read: BUILT BY JOHN D. ROCKEFELLER.

Rockefeller had apparently provided the funding to build that hospital in China, and decades later, Christine, among others, benefited from it. Giving lasts a very long time!

"A person lives as he invests himself in other's lives. A man is immortal as he is useful. He lives as long as the thing in which he has invested lives."

— *Ralph W. Stockman*

CHAPTER 5

Multiply Your Efforts

A non-profit organization called a few years ago and asked if Paul would support their ministry financially. He believed in what they were doing, but said, "No, I have a better idea."

He offered to pay the salary of a development director for two years who would in turn raise the funds the organization needed. They agreed, and by the time those two years had passed, the development director had raised 10 times what Paul was paying for his salary!

Talk about **multiplying** his efforts!

When Paul told me he was doing this, I thought, "That's absolutely brilliant!" The original gift keeps on giving and giving and giving.

Over the years, Paul and Jane have practiced this form of multiplication with more than 15 major charities and ministries, including Avance, Champions for Life, Lead Like Jesus, Friends for Life, Haggai Institute, Man in the Mirror, Marble Retreat, Marketplace Ministries Foundation, Mission Waco, Reach Out Youth Solutions, Ron Herrod Ministries, Texas Christian Academy, Waco Boys & Girls Club, among others.

Paying the development director's salary for the first year or two is like priming a pump. It has been an incredible thing to see, and these charities and ministries have raised millions upon millions of dollars thanks to Paul and Jane's initial gift and foresight.

Several years ago Paul met Inez Russell, an extremely dedicated woman whose passion is to help senior citizens who are not able to totally take care of themselves. With virtually no money and a handful of volunteers, she founded Friends for Life to stop abuse, neglect, and exploitation through legal guardianship, money management, and independent living programs. The people she helps are unable to perform daily tasks such as buying groceries, changing a light bulb, cleaning their home, or managing their bills.

After hearing her vision, Paul hired a development person for Friends for Life. The organization now has more than 2,000 volunteers to take care of 3,000 elderly people, and Friends for Life is ranked 11th out of thousands of charities in the United States for its overall organization and effectiveness. Her ministry is now used as a template for others throughout the nation. That is multiplication on top of multiplication!

Gil A. Stricklin, CEO of Marketplace Ministries Foundation relays another perfect example of making this approach work:

> The Meyers gave a one-time gift of $60,000 to help undergird the salary and/or development expenses for Marketplace Ministries. I have served as the founding president, CEO, and only development officer for the past eight years. His funds have assisted the ministry's growth from a few thousand dollars to a $5.2 million budget by the end of 2007.

This is quite a return on an initial investment anyway you look at it!

When you cannot serve to the degree that those you have helped are now serving others, you know you have multiplied yourself!

Multiply whatever you have

We all have different talents and abilities. Some have more, some have less, but this does not make one person better than another. We all need to understand two important facts:

- **First,** our natural gifts are just that, gifts, and they are from God; they are not self-generated.

- **Second,** God expects more from those who have been blessed with much.

Whatever it is that God has given us, His desire is that we use it wisely so that it multiplies.

Making multiplication commonplace

It's interesting to note that while multiplication is taught in school, it's rarely taught as a principle of real life. Whether that is due to mismanagement, pride, or lack of vision, multiplication is seldom experienced.

There are exceptions, however. One of the best examples of multiplication is that of the Haggai Institute. The concept of the institute's founder, John Edmund Haggai, is simple:

- train indigenous leaders how to reach their own people with the gospel of Jesus Christ, then

- train these Christian leaders how to equip other people for evangelism.

Since 1969, the Haggai Institute has trained over 75,000 indigenous Christian leaders in more than 180 different nations who, in turn, on average have each trained 100 more people. This has created the largest missionary force in the world, exceeding all Christian denominations combined!

Paul and Jane helped set up and fund a development department for the Haggai Institute in the 1980s, and the results since then have enabled the ministry to grow around the globe, and it's continuing to grow to this today.

Another example of multiplication is Baylor University in Waco, Texas. In 1963, university officials asked Paul to help with ideas on how to build their development department and expand Truett Seminary. Paul asked them to put together a map where all the alumni lived so that they could be used as contact points. Then, he asked them to produce a movie about the university, detailing its history, describing its current state, showcasing successful students, outlining its future plans, and presenting projected costs to accomplish their goals. The movie was shown to alumni all around the nation while recruiting fundraising developers and establishing campaigns to raise money.

> All prosperity begins in the mind and is dependent only on the full use of our creative imagination.
> — Ruth Ross

The effects of these ideas have compounded over the years, and Baylor has one of the top development teams of any university in America. The university's $30 million endowment has since increased to over $1 billion, making Baylor University one of the best-endowed private colleges in North America. Now that's multiplication!

Don't limit yourself

The first insurance company Paul worked for would not let him recruit other people, so he was limited by the hours he could work in a single day. So he left and joined another company that allowed him to recruit other salespeople, and you can bet he set the bar high. Paul recruited over 800 top sales agents. Needless to say, his career took off!

Multiplication may take longer than you plan as this anecdote illustrates: There once was a university in England partially enclosed by a stone wall. An ivy vine was planted beside the wall with hopes that the vine would grow and cover the wall, but after many years the ivy appeared dormant. Tired of waiting, the groundskeeper decided to give it one more year to grow.

The next year the ivy began to spread rapidly over the wall, covering it just as the groundskeeper envisioned. Out of curiosity, he gently dug around the plant and discovered one primary root that went directly toward a river located more than 70 feet away! All those years the ivy had been putting its entire effort into reaching the river. Once that was accomplished, multiplication took place at an alarming rate. Had the groundskeeper given up too quickly, multiplication would never have been realized.

LETTER OF THANKS

Dear Paul and Jane,

I am highly honored to be the first holder of the William M. Hinson Chair of Christian Scriptures, which you have made possible through your generous stewardship.

The wonderful thing about endowed chairs is that they will last as long as the institution is here. Buildings get torn down, but an endowed chair does not — it keeps on giving, and there will be many others to hold this chair down through the years.

We pray that we will do you honor for your incredible generosity, but far more importantly, bring glory to the Lord whom we both serve.

Blessings,
David E. Garland
William M. Hinson Chair of Christian Scriptures,
Associate Dean for Academic Affairs
George W. Truett Theological Seminary

Delay is part of the multiplication process. It takes time to get everything lined up, but once that occurs, watch out because things are about to erupt!

To multiply is to tap into your exponential potential. Here are the top six multipliers that I have learned from Paul Meyer's writing and his personal life:

#1 Multiplier — Connecting to God

The basis of all multiplication begins in a personal relationship with Jesus Christ. He has an infinite amount of everything you need, far more than you could handle at any one time.

It's like your house having the entire outflow of Hoover Dam's hydroelectric power plant at its disposal. There is no way you will ever be able to use the power behind the 17 generators inside the Hoover Dam because they have the capability of supplying all the electricity needed by a city of hundreds of thousands of people!

God living in you means that you are connected to the Creator of everything. By being plugged into Him, you truly have unlimited potential to grow, to increase, and to multiply.

Paul and Jane regularly pray and study the Bible together. It is during this time that inspiring ideas are conceived, that they are shown a particular path to take, or that they gain peace from a situation that has troubled them. Paul and Jane know that they are connected to the source of life — God Himself!

#2 Multiplier — Being Creative

We all have a God-given ability to be creative. Many of us have been told what we cannot do so often that we believe it to be true. Instead, we need to envision what we can do.

The ability to be creative is where potential and reality connect. You simply cannot be a multiplier if you are not creative. Creativity is a required ingredient.

Years ago, Paul purchased a farm in rural Texas. The ostrich business was booming at the time, so Paul converted his farm into an ostrich farm, and one year he made over $1 million in his venture. When ostrich farmers overpriced the eggs and chicks, the overall business went down and Paul got out of it.

But what to do now with his now-empty ostrich farm? Ever creative, Paul and Jane turned the entire farm into a Christian retreat and conference center. The empty ostrich coups with a single light bulb hanging from the ceiling are now beautiful rooms and lodges. If it weren't for the before and after pictures, you wouldn't believe it!

Today, his Summers Mill Retreat and Conference Center (www.summersmill.com) is a profitable venture that is providing benefits to countless people every day.

It all begins with stewardship and creativity.

LETTER OF THANKS

Dear Mr. Meyer,

I have stayed at your Summers Mill Retreat Center two separate times with the VA Leadership training. I just wanted to drop you a line to say how blessed I was to see such a retreat center being made available to the public. I spent several nights reading through a couple of your books that were in the room and was touched. Thank you so much for your vision and for following after the plan God designed for your life.

Paula K.

#3 Multiplier — Starting Small

It is virtually impossible to get what you want by waiting for it to fall into your lap. If you are not prepared to receive it, then you are not prepared to keep it. Starting small is therefore a good idea.

Years ago Paul invested in some educational software to help one child. The results were so favorable that the same software was introduced to other schools, resulting in more than 5,000 schools using this educational software today. The software company has now put 3.5 million kids through its software program for learning disabilities!

#4 Multiplier — Allowing Others to Give

Paul and Jane allow those who work for them in any of the Meyer Family Companies to give their time and expertise to charities on company time. The effect on his community has been phenomenal!

Paul and Jane will often give their time and energy in the form of the services of an executive staff member. It's a powerfully effective strategy. He explains the reasoning behind it:

> Take a city with approximately 200,000 people. Suppose the top 100 companies in that town had their top five people, spend 10 to 20% of their company time working in local charities, service organizations, or ministries. That would be 500 people. What would happen in that city? Think of the change of tone, of climate, of attitude. And what kind of percentages would you get? It would be incalculable, unbelievable.

A few years ago, Paul hosted an event with 24 select leaders. These businessmen were highly successful in their arenas, but they all took two days out of their schedules to meet with Paul. They wanted to know more about stewardship, about balancing life and success, and about keeping God the top focus of their lives.

Together in one of the buildings on Paul's Summers Mill property in Salado, Texas, Paul shared from his heart and invested in these 24 men whom he affectionately calls the "24 Warriors for Christ."

These men are continuing to put into practice what they learned, and the multiplying goes on.

#5 Multiplier — Learning to Delegate

Delegation sets the stage for multiplication. You can't do everything yourself. Think how limiting that can be! As you delegate, you will see a dramatic increase in your ability to dream, plan, and pursue other ideas.

Over a decade ago, Paul and Jane prayed that God would bring into their life the right person to become CEO of all the Meyer Family Companies and to also be president of the Paul and Jane Meyer Foundation. God answered that prayer through their daughter, Leslie, who introduced them to Terry and Brenda Irwin. Paul says that Terry is the best CEO he has had in their companies' history.

Each of the Meyer Family Companies has its own president who reports to Terry Irwin, which allows Paul and Jane the freedom to pursue what they feel called to do. Without the multiplying effects of delegation, they would both be hampered.

The final goal of multiplication

Multiplication is mathematically intended to do one thing: continue forever. Bringing in a lot of money, seeing a ministry grow rapidly, or watching something multiply at an exponential rate is always enjoyable, but that cannot be the ultimate goal.

In 1967, Paul wrote an article and then made a speech from it. He made an audio tape from the speech and sold a million copies. He was paid a royalty of 25 cents a piece. He took the tape and the profits and made a full-length training program from the principles outlined in the tape. Over the years, millions of dollars in royalties have come from that one program!

But Paul didn't stop there! He took the ongoing royalties and invested them in several foundations. Today that same money is still growing and will continue to grow indefinitely — all from an article he wrote in 1967!

Simply put: Multiply your ideas, your talent, and your money.

"The best investment with
the least risk and the
greatest dividend is giving."

— Sir John Templeton

CHAPTER **6**

Make No Excuses

Paul and Jane Meyer make no excuses about giving. It's who they are. It's what they do. Yet, if you ask the average person to give, you're more likely to get an excuse rather than money.

Most excuses, however, don't hold water. You'll see what I mean.

Excuse #1 — I can't afford to give right now.

Most of our unwillingness to give comes from this belief. We already feel stretched. We already go without things we'd like to have. We already feel guilty about asking our families to tighten their belts. Why complicate things by giving money away?

But bear in mind three important facts:

- *One, it's better to give a little than to give nothing at all.* And I mean better for you, as well as for others. You may start by setting aside what looks like an impossibly small amount, but merely by setting it aside, you gain a sense of control over your finances. You begin to grasp the discipline.

- *Two, there are few people so poor that they can't give at least a little.* Businessman Frank Madia began giving in his late teens when he received just $55 a week in the form of an unemployment check. He gave a tithe of 10%. Later, at age 40, Frank went into property development and raised the percentage to between 25 and 30%. **He saw the discipline of giving and his financial success as intimately connected.**

- *Three, it's a blatant reversal of the truth to say that giving keeps you poor.* Givers prosper! If you commit yourself to the discipline of giving, you will end up receiving more than you've given out.

Remember, giving is more investment than it is expenditure!

Most people have gotten into the habit of burdening themselves with debt repayment. They borrow, and as a result, the money they could have given or saved gets paid to their creditors as interest.

The truth is, it has very little to do with our income level and more to do with our spending patterns.

The concept we have had in America for a number of years now is that it doesn't matter if you spend 105% of what you make, because next year you're going to get a 10% raise, and it will take care of itself. The problem is that next year you spend 105% again, and the debt continues to go up.

Excuse #2 — My little bit will make no difference.

A lot of people think, "When I'm worth millions, I'll give, too." But reality is this: The little amounts that we give are what enable charities and ministries to meet their needs.

One Sunday afternoon in the 1880s, a six-year-old girl by the name of Hattie Wiatt got turned away from the Sunday school at Grace Baptist Church on Berks and Mervine Streets in Philadelphia. The church occupied a small site, many families attended, and the Sunday school classes were full. Bitterly disappointed, Hattie resolved that, if she could not attend the existing Sunday school, she would save her pennies and build a new one.

Hattie picked out a small red purse, and every week put into it a large portion of her pocket money. Not long afterward, she became seriously ill, but before she died she told her mother about the purse, and made her mother promise to give the money to Grace Baptist Church on the condition that it be used only for the purpose she intended.

The purse contained just 57 cents.

The next Sunday, the minister, Dr. Russell Conwell relayed this information to a silent congregation.

"When we heard how God had blessed us with so great an inheritance," said a member of the congregation later, "there was silence — the silence of tears and earnest consecration. We felt that the cornerstone of a new church was laid."

Hattie Wiatt's tiny legacy precipitated the church's decision to build, not just a new Sunday school, but a whole new complex. This was no light task. The congregation consisted mostly of working men and women who could not afford to make large donations to a building fund. But Hattie Wiatt's example inspired them to save.

Tired men, muscles aching from a hard day's work, and women weary from a long day spent at a typewriter or a shop counter, cheerfully trudged home on foot to save the nickels. They gave up smoking and gave their tobacco money. They stayed home over summer and gave their vacation money. Innumerable entertainments were held. A fair was put on in one of the largest halls of Philadelphia, in the central part of the city, attracting thousands of visitors and netting nearly $9,000.

LETTER OF THANKS

Mr. Meyer sought me out several years ago with a simple request, "May we help you with your ministry?" And help he did. The Paul and Jane Meyer Family Foundation lovingly began to help us acquire each item on our long list of equipment needs.

The foundation helped us purchase two big Class 8 tractors, three huge van trailers, and our fork-lift. They have also provided us with much needed warehouse space and regular monthly support.

Because of Paul and Jane, we are able to minister to tens of thousands of people annually. I am amazed at the wonderful things that can be accomplished when one couple decides to say, "Yes, Lord."

Rick Caywood
President, Rick Caywood Ministries

Finally, in September 1886, they purchased the lot at Broad and Berks Streets for $25,000. Ground for the church was broken March 27, 1889, and the cornerstone was laid July 13, 1890.

A few years later on that very site stood the Baptist Temple of Philadelphia.

"**During the opening exercises, over 9,000 people were present at each service,**" said the *Philadelphia Press*, describing the opening. "The very air seemed to thrill with thanksgiving that day." As well it should.

The down payment on the site? Just 57 cents!

The power of this story, of course, rests on the courage of a small child. The principle it embodies — of the exemplary power of giving — stands true for adults, as much as for children.

It also shows clearly how an apparently impossible goal can be achieved on the strength of small donations.

Ask fundraisers. You won't find one of them who will snub a $5 gift. In many cases, it's the $5 gifts that support million-dollar projects.

Excuse #3 — I'm not capable of big donations.

It's not about making big donations … it's about *making* a donation. Though the media will report a $2 million gift, you'll never hear about the many people who gave $25 to a local charity that feeds the poor.

The truth is, most charities will never get a $2 million windfall! They need the small amounts because it's those amounts that pay the bills, feed the poor, and shelter the homeless.

> He who bestows his goods upon the poor shall have as much again, and 10 times more.
> — John Bunyan

Once and for all, remove the thought that only big donations "count." Every dollar counts!

Then in the future when you have more, give more. It's as easy as that.

Excuse #4 — I can't afford to tithe.

Paul and Jane have counseled numerous individuals and families over the years, trying to help them sort out their financial situations. The first thing they say is, "If you aren't tithing, you will begin tithing right now. If you don't honor God with your money, there is nothing I can do to help you."

John D. Rockefeller, for instance, tithed while he was an assistant bookkeeper earning a very meager amount! He said, "I never would have been able to tithe the first million dollars I ever made if I had not tithed my first salary, which was $1.50 per week."

Tithing is more than a discipline. It is a statement of your faith in God — it is you choosing to give rather than take, and it is a key that opens doors of blessing into your life.

I've seen it countless times where people started to tithe and business opportunities suddenly appeared in front of them. Looking at the stories, you would agree that it's nothing less than miraculous.

LETTER OF THANKS

Mr. Meyer,

I just want to thank you for the ramp. I appreciate it so much. They did such a good job on it.

At least I feel a little more mobile now that I can take my chair outside.

Someday I will get a scooter that I can take to the store with me. My chair is too heavy to lift in and out.

God bless you!
Judy B.

The question is not whether you can afford to tithe. It is whether you can afford not to.

What's more, the Bible talks more about money than any other subject, so it can be assumed that money is very important to God, and therefore to us!

Excuse #5 — I might be taken advantage of.

Paul was putting gas in his airplane one day when a boy came up and said, "I've been wanting to thank you."

Not recognizing him, Paul said, "For what?"

"I did you a favor four years ago by taking care of your airplane. I didn't tell you then, but I had just quit school. You gave me a hundred bucks and thanked me for taking care of the plane. I used that money to buy some schoolbooks that same afternoon. I felt God was telling me to go back to school. I graduated, and now I have a job with a petroleum company. It would have never happened if it were not for your $100."

Some say that the more generous you are the more easily you will be taken for a ride. That very question arose during an executive training session that my wife Bettye and I, along with Paul and Jane, hosted at their Summers Mill Retreat and Conference Center. Somebody asked Jane if anyone ever took advantage of Paul, and how she felt about it.

Jane candidly replied, "Yes, it does happen. It used to make me mad, but Paul always tells me that it doesn't really matter and that the important thing is for him to be doing things for people. Yes, he gets taken advantage of, but he's OK with that."

Paul and Jane don't worry if occasionally, and it's *only* occasionally, they get taken advantage of in this life. They know they are laying up treasure in heaven for their faithfulness and generosity. That's plenty good enough for Paul and Jane!

Givers always win in the end. You can take that to the bank!

"It's OK to have wealth. But keep it in your hands, not in your heart."

— *S. Truett Cathy*

========= CHAPTER 7 =========

Stewardship of Yourself

Stewardship requires that you be a good steward ... of yourself. So, wherever you are, whatever you do, you are being a steward of yourself.

Begin with your priorities

Your priorities define you. They say who you are and what you believe is most important. If you haven't already done so, take some time to write down your priorities.

Here are Paul and Jane's priorities:
1. God
2. Each other
3. Family
4. Health and fitness
5. Business

The natural next step is, of course, to live out those priorities, which is the true test of anyone's stewardship of self.

Stick to your guns

It seems that as soon as you take a stand, something or someone comes along to challenge you. That is certainly the case in the area of stewardship.

Many years ago, soon after Paul made the commitment to start tithing 10% of his income, the company he worked for went out of business. The business failure had nothing to do with Paul, but some people might be inclined to say, "Well, I'll just hold onto my money. Tithing isn't helping at all."

But Paul kept up the habit of tithing. He didn't quit. I was there. I watched him do it.

When business turned around, he began to increase his giving, bit by bit. Paul started down the path of stewardship and chose to remain true to his commitment, regardless of anything that happened.

> I have made many millions, but they have brought me no happiness.
> — John D. Rockefeller, Sr.

Paul's income, by the way, has rocked upward since that time. Imagine making a product that didn't just make millions, or tens of millions, but hundreds of millions of dollars in sales. Paul ha done that multiple times.

I've watched it happen over the years, and it's been fun to watch. Paul's and Jane's giving increases as they go.

Today, sadly, many people practice situational ethics. They let the situations guide them rather than living according to their priorities. In the end, they don't know who they are or what they believe.

But as a steward, you must stick to your guns. You know exactly who you are, what you believe, and where you are going, and that is a powerful, yet peaceful, place to be.

Be true to yourself

Many years ago Paul was asked to visit a 26-year-old man who was hospitalized with bleeding ulcers. After briefly getting acquainted, Paul looked him in the eye and asked, "*If you had nobody to please in life, what would you do?*"

The young man immediately started to cry like a child. Through tears, he sobbed, "I have always wanted to be a farmer."

Instead of pursuing his lifelong passion, he was in college working toward a degree he knew he didn't want to use! It was a nightmare for him, each day enduring a life he hated living. "He was a square peg in a round hole — the proverbial fish out of water — to a degree that I had never witnessed before!," Paul said.

Paul told him he needed to call in his family who loved him and who were concerned about him, but who thought they knew what was better for his life than he did. Paul told the young man to tell his family that he could no longer live the life they were planning for him. He was trying hard to be somebody he was not out of a misguided sense of obedience and love for his parents and family, but it was *his* life and he wanted to be the one writing the story.

From his hospital bed, the young man told his family what had been on his heart for so many years, *and they finally understood!*

Having made that decision, the healing process began immediately. The doctor attending him said that within 24 hours of the family confrontation, the young man's ulcers suddenly stopped bleeding!

Until then the ulcers were out of control — the doctors had tried everything and nothing could stop the bleeding! In no time at all, the young man walked out of the hospital, never to return to the hospital or to any college campus again.

Today he is a farmer, owns a feed store, has a wife and children, and is living a life he always wanted to live.

Each of us needs to be able to say, with boldness, "I am a good steward. I am using the talents and abilities that God gave me to their fullest potential."

LETTER OF THANKS

Dear Mr. Meyer,

I wanted to take this opportunity to sincerely thank you for your financial help and making my nursing education possible. I met you for the first and only time a couple of years ago when you came in to see Dr. Sterriker.

We visited for about 20 minutes and then you offered me your card and your financial help for my educational expenses. That day became a turning point in my life. I truly believe it was God's intention for our paths to cross.

I graduated from college and passed my nursing boards and now I am a registered nurse. I hope I am able to make a difference in my patients' lives and pass on the same positive attitude that you have shown to me.

Sharon S.

If you run a business

If you own or operate a business, you are to be a steward of your employees, in addition to being a steward of the business and its customers.

When one of Paul's employees asks for time off for some special trip with their spouse, Paul always says, "Go. Time with your spouse is more important than anything you're doing here." Boy, does that create loyalty.

And if someone isn't performing, Paul explains:

I don't fire people when they don't do a good job. If a person isn't performing well, I get some other people together and form a committee. I say, "We're not going to fire you. We're going to give you this support. You can borrow this brainpower until you can get back on track. When you get back on track, then they will disband and leave you on your own again." I don't know why more companies don't do that. They will fire a person who has made one mistake, when he's doing ninety percent a good job.

I remember well that several years ago, one of Paul's top executives had a big financial problem. Paul and a colleague helped sort out all his problems, and in short order, the executive was back on track financially.

Anytime you can make life better for employees, they will run the business better, watch the money better, be more creative, make more sales, and just do what it takes to be a loyal employee. It's a win-win benefit of stewardship in business.

If you are a leader

Paul believes that everyone is a leader to some degree or another, so wherever you lead, you are to serve. That is because leaders who serve create greater creativity, a happier working atmosphere, stronger unity, and higher profits.

People work harder when the leader serves them, and that makes you want to serve them even more. People are then more committed and more willing to grow, and thus, the cycle continues.

> Let him who exhorts others to give, give himself.
> — Latin Proverb

The late Cecil Day, one of the most respected businessmen of all time and the founder of Days Inns, was a servant leader. During the Arab oil embargo of the early '70s, he cut his salary to $100 a week — and he did this for a year and a half! He did everything he could to keep the paychecks coming to his employees.

It is not a legal requirement for you to apply these principles of service, but I do believe it is a moral requirement for those who choose to be stewards.

It is also a great way to treat people!

Jesus went so far as to say, *"If anyone wants to be first, he must be the very last, and the servant of all"* (Mark 9:35). Being a steward is all about service.

> A deal is only a deal when it's a good deal for both parties (spoken before paying a farmer twice the asking price for his property).
> — Cecil B. Day, founder of Days Inns

After training, teaching, and encouraging his disciples, Jesus washed their feet — a statement of humility that few today would ever make — then he went even further and died on the cross for them!

We can't top His act of service, but it stands as a stark reminder to us of how much service we can give.

Service is the mark of a steward.

If you have a heart for evangelism

When Paul was 24 years old and excelling in the insurance business, I invited him to a meeting with about 40 of North America's most influential business leaders, including Rev. Billy Graham.

Rev. Graham asked if anyone had any questions. Paul asked, "Why did God call my pastor into ministry and not me?"

"What do you do?" Rev. Graham asked.

"I sell life insurance," Paul replied.

"Are you good at it?"

"Yes, you could say I am." At that time, Paul led the entire nation in life insurance sales, setting records that have still not been beaten.

The famous preacher continued, "Young man, God's will for your life might be to make money. You just need to be obedient to do what He has equipped and enabled you to do; that is your ministry."

The comment brought great liberty to Paul's heart and soul. He was freed from thinking that he should be doing something more "meaningful." Instead, he could focus on what God had for him to do.

Making money, it turned out, was only a small part of what God had planned for Paul, for over the years, thousands of people have come to know Jesus as a result of Paul's work.

Author Patrick Morley notes that, "95% of us will never be in 'occupational' ministry," but he is quick to add, "That does not mean we are not ministers." Paul has certainly taken this to heart!

Look for stewardship opportunities

I read about a man who was looking for a new job. He had an appointment across town, traffic was bad, and he was trying hard not to be late. Just then he noticed a woman on the side of the road looking at her car's flat tire.

The question, "Should I stop or not?" briefly went through his mind, and then he pulled over to help.

The woman was dressed nicely, and obviously heading to work. The man changed her tire as quickly as he could and she went on her way. He wiped the grime off his hands and headed to his appointment — already late.

When the man arrived at his appointment, he apologized profusely. He was ushered into the room of the human resources director, who happened to be the very woman whose tire he had changed just 30 minutes earlier.

Needless to say, he got the job!

LETTER OF THANKS

Dear Mr. and Mrs. Meyer,

You probably are not aware of this, but two years ago, you and Jane so generously contacted us to indicate your desire to match the contributions to the Feast of Caring. Last year we continued it, and are hopeful of continuing it again this year.

Your exceptional gift meant that we experienced the most successful Feast of Caring ever from a fundraising perspective, raising over $80,000 for the support of the ministry and mission of Caritas.

Gratefully,
Kenneth Moerbe
Caritas

Sometimes it's the little things that prove to be the big things. You never know what someone is going through, and your "little" gift of a coffee, a word of encouragement, letter, or recommendation, might be an absolutely huge gesture for the other person.

Several years ago, Paul met a man who was facing increased health problems and a business that he could not handle. With only a meager retirement, the man was in trouble.

Paul took a little time and advised him how to use his business to fund his retirement. The much-needed advice proved to be the answer to his dilemma and the man is now retired and financially set for the rest of his life.

Because Paul is always looking for ways to help other people, he saw this opportunity and took it. That is a natural part of being a steward.

Have fun helping others

A few years ago, Paul heard a woman talk about domestic violence. She had been violently abused, yet she was speaking to several hundred people, telling how she had recovered and was moving on.

"She had incredible grit and determination and an attitude that was absolutely wonderful," Paul says, "but her teeth were a complete mess. Something needed to be done."

When the meeting was over, the woman was talking with people as she walked toward the back door. Paul met her and whispered in her ear, "If you would be willing, I would like to pay to have your teeth worked on by a dentist."

She started to cry right there on the spot, and she agreed to it.

Not only do Paul and Jane enjoy helping other people, but they also recognize that it is their responsibility to do so. James 4:17 explains, *"To him who knows to do good and does not do it, to him it is a sin."*

This, I believe, is because God has plans for each one of us, things that He can only accomplish through us. Scripture says that we were created, *"to do good works, which God prepared in advance for us to do"* (Ephesians 2:10).

I read that Abraham Lincoln was once strolling through town when he saw a slave girl being sold at auction. He entered the bidding and purchased the girl. Her first question to her new master was "What are you going to do with me?"

Lincoln replied, "Set you free."

When she realized that she could do what she wanted, wear what she wanted, say what she wanted, and go where she wanted, she was speechless. Lincoln asked her, "What are you going to do now?"

She immediately replied, "Go with you."

Instead of complaining, arguing, or making a commotion at the auction, Lincoln simply took action. In addition to being a steward, I bet Lincoln and his staff enjoyed changing that girl's life!

A steward, I believe, lives a very gratifying and fulfilling life. I would say that Paul and Jane Meyer are the very embodiment of stewardship.

"Ordinary riches can be stolen, real riches cannot. In your soul are infinitely precious things that cannot be taken from you."

— *Oscar Wilde*

CHAPTER 8

Stewardship Toward God

What you believe determines what you do with your life. The same is true for everyone.

But here's the deal: God loves us, He has great things in store for us, and He has made a way for us to be reconciled to Him.

Our act of stewardship toward God is to take Him up on His offer. Eternal life is no small matter!

But can you trust God?

Trusting God requires two choices that no one can make but you. The first decision is the most important one:

#1 — Do you trust God with your eternity?

When Paul was just 16 years old and standing alone in a vineyard, he made that decision, and it changed his whole life, and the lives of countless others he would assist through decades of philanthropy.

Jesus said, *"I am the door: If anyone enters by me, he will be saved"* (John 10:9). Though his mother led him to that door, Paul made the willful choice to confess his sins and ask Jesus into his heart. We must each do the same.

#2 — Do you trust God with your daily life?

Eternity is forever, while a mere 70 to 90 years on earth is nothing more than a drop in an ocean-sized bucket. Why are we quick to trust God with our eternity, yet we struggle with trusting Him in our daily lives?

What would cause a person not to trust God? After all, He is never late, never unfaithful, never cruel, never absent, never unloving, and never wrong. Have we been preconditioned to believe otherwise?

If you, like me, have had plenty of trust-defeating experiences, don't hold that against God. We can trust God because He is *"a God of truth and without injustice; righteous and upright is He"* (Deuteronomy 32:4) who desires that we experience *"life, and that they may have it more abundantly"* (John 10:10).

Loving God

God doesn't offer only a few select people the opportunity to know Him. Instead, He wants to have a personal relationship with everyone, but He will never impose.

Is it possible to know God like you know your best friend? Yes, though you obviously cannot sit down with God and have a cup of coffee together. The relationship is different, yet it's the same — but better!

Going for a walk with someone is one method to get to know that person. What you do is not as important as the fact that you are listening and seeking to understand each other.

Christians have sought to know God for generations, often by asking questions like: "How many chapters do I need to read in the Bible? How long should I pray? What happens if I miss one day? Is 10 minutes long enough?"

Such questions miss the point. They focus on the <u>method</u>, which is legalistic and will stifle any relationship, instead of the <u>reason</u>. You spend time with someone because you want to, not because you are ordered to. In relation to God, your love for Him is not limited to something like an emotional high from a certain experience. You are to love Him with everything you are, wholly and completely.

> It's not how much we give but how much love we put into giving.
> — Mother Teresa

The more you love, the more you know Him — and the more you know Him, the more you love.

Praying to God

We must believe that God hears, that He cares, and that He acts on our behalf. That is faith. For prayer to be effective, faith is required. Without faith, prayer accomplishes virtually nothing … but with faith, anything is possible!

Jesus said, *"Ask, and it will be given to you; seek and you will find; knock, and it will be opened to you"* (Matthew 7:7).

As long as Paul and I have been friends — I first met him when he was just 23 years old — I know he believes strongly in the power of prayer and stresses its importance for direction, strength, peace, and joy. He opens his day with, **"This is the day that the Lord has made. Let us rejoice and be glad in it**." Then he adds, **"Show me who I can minister to today**." My, but has God answered that request in Paul's life!

Jesus prayed, *"Not my will, but yours be done"* (Luke 22:42). His purpose was to accomplish God's will. I have the same purpose, ***as does every Christian***, which means my prayers ought to be for what He has for me to do, not for my own selfish desires.

Several years ago Paul wanted to set up a program to help the economically-disadvantaged youth in his town go to college. In prayer, God revealed to him an innovative way to make the vision a reality. As a result, the Passport to Success Foundation was established as the financial vehicle to make this possible.

LETTER OF THANKS

Dear Paul and Jane,

Thank you for your generous pledge of support for a Development Director and for your donation! Your contribution makes it possible for Champions for Life to continue ministering in prisons, schools, and to youth at risk.

Since the beginning of this ministry, we have reached out to millions of inmates and countless thousands of youth, all for the purpose of doing as the Lord commanded — fulfilling the Great Commission.

We plan on growing and reaching thousands more for Christ. This is only possible because of thoughtful contributions from people like you. We are blessed to call you friend.

In Him as always,
Bill Glass
Champions for Life

This inspired other Waco, Texas, families to start their own programs, including the foundations of Malcolm and Mary Ruth Duncan, Bernard and Audre Rapoport, and Clifton and Betsy Robinson. The combined efforts of these foundations have already helped over 6,000 disadvantaged youth in Paul's county attend college!

In addition, if Paul says he is going to pray for you, know that he will. A lot of people talk about praying, but not that many people commit to prayer. I've been very impressed over the years with Paul and Jane's follow-through in this area, and it speaks volumes about their walk with God, their trust, and their commitment as stewards.

Obeying God

It won't take much time in prayer before you discover another vital ingredient of prayer: obedience. When He speaks, we are to obey, even if it doesn't make sense. Obedience protects, directs, and catapults us to heights we could never have imagined otherwise.

When you make Him Lord of your life, you give up the right to say "no" to His commands. When He speaks, you obey. That is where growth, breakthrough, and blessing take place.

Paul shared with me a story that illustrates this point so well.

> I had an especially pivotal breakthrough in my knowledge of God. I had invested a lot of time, energy, and money into a business venture that was ready to be launched. However, I suddenly found myself in a difficult situation: proceed against my morals and business ethics based on God's Word or let the business die at the starting gate. I chose the second option. Within days I was offered an opportunity that eventually led me to where I am today. Through that experience I came to understand that God was even more interested in my welfare than I was! By obeying Him, I benefited in every way.

Serving God

Serving God is the last part of knowing Him. People who place serving first often accomplish great things for God, but many fail to have a personal relationship with Him along the way. It's about *being* before *doing*.

Scripture plainly states, *"And this is eternal life, that they may know You, the only true God, and Jesus Christ whom You have sent"* (John 17:3). Since knowing God is eternal life, it makes sense that we should focus on knowing God rather than on serving Him.

This by no means minimizes the importance of serving. We usually end up serving Him as a result of obedience. Some of the most meaningful and enjoyable times in life have come as I obeyed God by serving others.

Happiness that comes through service that originated in obedience is so intense that words can't describe it! You will have to experience it for yourself!

All of this is such an integral part of stewardship.

"You can make a difference
if you link your life to a
worthy institution that
will live on when
you are gone."

— *Olan Hugh Runnels*

CHAPTER 9

The Mission of Paul & Jane Meyer

Several years ago Paul was invited to lecture to all of the business and administration students at a large university. I was privileged to accompany him for his lecture.

After the dean of the school of business administration gave him a positive introduction enumerating Paul's great successes in business, Paul opened his lecture by listing the number of his business failures and naming some of them.

His speech was much more effective as he told them he had started more than 100 companies, with a failure rate of around 70%. He likes to give those statistics to encourage others not to give up when obstacles present themselves or when plans are derailed. After all, 30% of his businesses did go on to be a success.

Over the past 20 years, a larger percentage of their income has gone directly into the Paul and Jane Meyer Family Foundation to perpetuate the charities and ministries they support.

The Meyers have already started this process. Many of the family-owned companies are managed by a trustee group, some have been gifted and turned over to individuals, and others are in trust for the Meyer children.

Paul's goal is actually to die broke — to give away all his wealth! His strong belief is summed up in the words of Andrew Carnegie who said, "A man who dies rich dies in disgrace."

Paul and Jane believe that certain Scriptures are directed toward people whom God has blessed with prosperity. One Scripture that has particularly influenced them is 1 Timothy 6:17-19, which says,

> ***Command those who are rich in this present age not to be haughty, nor to trust in uncertain riches, but in the living God, who gives us richly all things to enjoy. Let them do good, that they be rich in good works, ready to give, willing to share, storing up for themselves a good foundation for the time to come, that they may lay hold on eternal life.***

This Scripture and others related to giving support Paul and Jane's sense of responsibility to share their abundant blessings. They truly embrace the belief that it is more blessed to give than to receive, and they are firmly committed to that precept.

Two main themes arise over and over when Paul talks about giving. He wants to multiply his giving and create a process of perpetual giving.

The Paul and Jane Meyer Family Foundation

The foundation's mission, which was written by Jane, is as follows:

Our Mission

*To follow the principle that the
Christian life is a service life.*

Our Mission Statement

*To provide resources to carry out
the work of the Great Commission
by investing in Christian mission
ministries, charities and needed
individuals, that they might in turn,
impact our world for Jesus Christ.
The Paul and Jane Meyer Family Foundation
is a Christ-Centered foundation
established to financially assist the
youth, elderly, and needy in
Central Texas, and occasionally
on a selective global basis.*

It has been Paul and Jane's desire to multiply their blessings in every way possible by establishing ministries of their own, as well as supporting countless ministries that effectively meet the needs of the disadvantaged while spreading the Gospel of Jesus Christ.

Paul and Jane's efforts have even reached an international level. Having done business in Japan for some 35 years, Paul explains, "We love the Japanese people. Many years ago while in Japan, I prayed with Jane and our daughter Leslie, 'Thank you God for all the success we've had here in Japan but I'd trade it all if I could lead one of these Shinto Buddhists to Christ.'"

About 30 minutes later on the way to a meeting, James Mundai, their Japanese translator, who was a local pastor, started to cry. He sobbed, "Why would God make a fool out of me? I've been here 27 years and not one person has accepted Christ. What is your answer to that, Paul?"

"It's all in God's timing," Paul replied.

That day at the meeting, Paul was asked to speak about what was important to him. Although he was a bit nervous, Paul decided to talk about his relationship with Jesus. Then he said to the group, "I can't explain it all as well as James Mundai can, so I would like for him to speak."

In that room of 35 people, 17 accepted Jesus as their personal Savior.

The next night at another meeting a woman stood up and asked Paul, "Do you love your wife?" Paul replied that he did, and the woman asked him to tell Jane right there that he loved her. So Paul said very clearly, "Jane, I love you." There was an immediate standing ovation!

Then someone asked, "What is your greatest motivation?"

Paul replied, "My greatest motivation is my Lord and Savior, Jesus Christ. If you want to know more, come and hear my friend James Mundai speak tonight." That night even more people became Christians.

Hundreds of Paul's companies' clients in Japan have become Christians. James Mundai went on to build a seven-story high church in Matsuya, Japan.

Living out the mission

To both encourage and inspire you, allow me to introduce you to just a few of the many incredible ministries founded or supported by Paul and Jane Meyer:

#1
The Paul and Jane Meyer Family Foundation

In 1984, the **Paul and Jane Meyer Family Foundation** was established based on strong Christian values, and with the explicit intent of building the groundwork for perpetual giving. From the beginning, the foundation's primary focus has been to provide that which is missing in the lives of the economically-disadvantaged, the physically challenged, the elderly, and those lacking sufficient education.

Realizing the difficulty for any single entity to be the best at everything, the foundation has often united with other local foundations and concerned individuals to combine talents and become the best at virtually everything.

Championing the strength of this unity and maintaining a strong belief in "leverage and multiplication," the foundation encourages other organizations, charities, and individuals to set up foundations and endowments to perpetuate their ministries.

As a result, what started as a goal to help local citizens become proud of their community, ultimately has affected people globally. In reality, it would be impossible to count the people that have been both touched and rewarded by the partnerships and associations created through this planned unity.

#2
The Haggai Institute

The Haggai Institute is the very example that characterizes Paul and Jane Meyer's commitment to world evangelism. **For that reason, the institute is the No. 1 recipient of funds from the Paul and Jane Meyer Family Foundation, with gifts exceeding $14 million to date.**

Established in 1969 by John Edmund Haggai, The Haggai Institute is an international and interdenominational organization founded to equip Asian, African, and Latin American Christian leaders with the skills to train others to reach their own people for Christ.

The numerous international institutes enroll Christian leaders in their programs to train them how to teach others about the Gospel. More than 76,000 leaders have been trained through the Haggai Institute program. They are evangelizing and training others in 178 countries and territories on six continents.

#3
Friends for Life

This model facility, which is the brainchild and dream of **Friends for Life** founder, Inez Russell, is the home of an adult daycare center, an early childhood center, and administrative offices for all the many services offered to help the elderly and adults with disabilities in Central Texas. Friends for Life has grown and expanded its services to include **The Meyer Family Intergenerational Center**.

The expansive new center features a library, music room, computer lab, garden area, and an arts and crafts area where older adults and children span the generations to interact with each other. The center also houses the offices that administer a legal guardianship program and a money management program.

In addition, on the grounds of the Friends for Life campus you will find **Allie's Place**, a play area dedicated in memory of Allison Ann Bucy, or "Allie" as she was affectionately known. Allie was the daughter of the Honorable Judge Jim and Carolyn Meyer, and the granddaughter of Paul and Jane Meyer and Jim and Helen Cole. She died at the age of 23 from Vascular Ehlers-Danlos Syndrome (EDS).

#4
Mission Waco

Through **The Meyer Center for Urban Ministries**, the poor and marginalized can find opportunities for empowerment and personal development from the services offered through 26 different ministries and programs. The Meyer Center offers the following programs and services:

- MPowerment, a job training program,
- My Brother's Keeper, a shelter for homeless men,
- The Meyer Center Community Clinic,
- Manna House, a drug/alcohol outreach program, and
- GED classes.

#5
The Carpenter's Hammer Ministry

This is one of the many ministries actually started by Paul and Jane based on Paul's encounter with a young man in a wheel chair. It provides emergency repair service for elderly, disabled, and shut-ins.

Among the repairs the ministry has provided are construction of wheelchair ramps, installation of grasp bars in bathrooms, roof replacements, and other home repairs. More than 200 homes have been given an overhaul or ramps.

#6
Family Abuse Center

The **Meyer Center for Domestic Violence** provides a safe haven for victims of domestic violence and offers 24-hour emergency shelter, legal advocacy, case management, a 24-hour crisis hotline, residential and non-residential group and individual counseling, parenting skills, and Start First, an education/intervention program. It has received national praise as "a model of how to do it right."

#7
Summers Mill Retreat and Conference Center

Paul and Jane started this ministry in 1998. Summers Mill is a full-service retreat and conference center located in Central Texas. Its serene, rural location near the meandering Salado Creek is the perfect setting for small and large groups that want a first-class conference facility with a comfortable, down home feel.

Accommodations, which can house up to 200 people, consist of lodges and guesthouses, enhancing the natural atmosphere. The center also boasts a state-of-the-art exercise and recreation facility, as well as a baseball field and walking trails. But it is the center's meeting facilities that rank among the best in Texas.

8
Rick Caywood Ministries

This ministry enlists a small army of paid and volunteer truckers to traverse the country each week using a fleet of 18-wheelers, picking up loads of low-cost dry goods in locations across the United States. The goods are then delivered to Mexico or to the rural South to feed the needy.

The ministry partners with about 100 other Christian ministries of various denominations to distribute the items. Each year thousands of poor people receive food supplies like pinto beans, potatoes, and powdered milk. Annually, they give away and deliver several million pounds of mostly donated food and relief products valued at well into the tens of millions of dollars.

The ever-optimistic founder Rick Caywood points out, "We are in our 12th year of fulfilling our mission to feed God's children in all the nations, all the world, all Creation, and to the uttermost parts of the earth."

#9
The Meyer Center for Christian Studies at University of Mary Hardin-Baylor

When officials at the University of Mary Hardin-Baylor in Belton, Texas, announced the establishment of the College of Christian

Studies in June 2003, they knew demand for courses in Christian studies was on the rise. Besides their projected increase in enrollment, the university required all students to take Old and New Testament Survey, making sufficient classroom space even more critical.

The answer to their quandary came in the form of a $1 million grant from the Paul and Jane Meyer Family Foundation toward the $4.1 million project to build a 18,815 square-foot, two-story building (completed in 2008) that houses five classrooms, conference rooms, the dean's office, faculty offices, a reading room, a lounge area, and a chapel.

Christian Studies students will be able to complete 39 hours in their Christian Studies majors with classes offered in:

- Biblical Studies
- Church History
- Christian Ministry
- Theology
- Christian Studies
- Philosophy

#10
Passport to Success Foundation, Inc.

Founded in 1988 by Paul and Jane Meyer, the Passport to Success scholarship program provides funds for economically-disadvantaged students in Central Texas so that they can attend college with the help of grants and/or no-interest loans.

Paul and Jane Meyer have contributed over $8 million to Passport to Success Foundation, Inc. They have also combined resources with Malcolm and Ruth Duncan (through the MAC Grant Program), the Bernard and Audre Rapoport Foundation, and the Clifton and Betsy Robinson Foundation to help more than 6,000 students obtain higher education.

#11
Central Texas Astronomical Society

The Paul and Jane Meyer Observatory in Clifton, Texas, offers students the opportunity to study the heavens. Thanks to the generous donation from the foundation, the astronomical society was able to purchase a robotic, research grade 24-inch telescope.

The telescope is considered to be as good as any telescope found at the McDonald Observatory in the Davis Mountains of West Texas; it just happens to be smaller.

Data gathered at the observatory is shared with other organizations to further the science of astronomy. Data also can be sent via the Internet to Central Texas schools to facilitate science classes that are focusing on astronomy.

LETTER OF THANKS

Mr. Meyer,

I would like to express how much I appreciate your support of my education at MCC through the Passport to Success program.

Your generosity of this gift will never be forgotten and I hope to someday pass this opportunity forward to another individual in honor of your philanthropic way.

Sincerely,
Deborah A.

#12
Lead Like Jesus

The Lead Like Jesus ministry, founded in 1999 by Ken Blanchard and Phil Hodges, is committed to creating a world where leaders of organizations, no matter how large or small, more closely reflect the leadership style of the greatest leader of all time, Jesus of Nazareth.

Paul and Jane Meyer strongly believe that the programs offered by Lead Like Jesus are greatly needed in many of today's businesses, as it seems more and more leaders face an upward trend in unprincipled business practices. To help reverse the trend, the Meyer Family Foundation, along with the Gary and Diane Heavin Foundation, have committed substantial support to the Lead Like Jesus ministry.

Through the ministry's Leadership Encounter program, people of faith, or anyone else searching for a relevant and effective model for their own day-to-day leadership, take an enlightening and life-changing look at Jesus as a role model. The dynamic workshop closely examines Jesus as a leader and a model while equipping participants to lead as He led.

Deciding where to give

The previous list is comprised of just 12 of the 55 major ministries the Meyer's support with contributions ranging from over $3 million to $50,000, along with more than 300 ministries that have received smaller contributions of under $50,000, for a grand total of more than $65 million dollars in contributions since 1984.

When asked how he decides where to give, Paul replies, "I ask myself where would Christ be today if He were in town? Who would He help? Who would He talk to? I believe those are the places we need to be all the time, not just at Christmas time."

The Meyers truly believe, "We bring nothing into this world and we take nothing out. We are stewards of what we have or accumulate. The purpose of living is to give, to share, to multiply ourselves mentally, spiritually, and materially."

There's no doubt they are doing just that!

Where are you going to give? What is the next charity, ministry, or person you will support?

"Wealth is a responsibility
and the sharing of it
a way of life."

— *Peter Haas, Jr.*

CHAPTER 10

Perpetual Stewardship

A child sits at a computer keyboard with earphones on. On the screen the image of a golden retriever flashes.

"Dog," says the voice from the computer. "D-o-g. Dog. Say dog."

"Dog," the child says.

"Now type 'dog.'"

The child types it, but incorrectly: d-o-t.

"Good try. Try again."

All the responses are positive. The child sees; the child hears; the child acts. The program works on all three ways people process information: visual, auditory, and kinesthetic.

This is unusual. In the typical classroom, attention and praise focus on the students who learn by hearing and seeing. Students who learn kinesthetically — by doing — often become marginalized and disadvantaged.

This software comes from one of Paul's companies: the Creative Education Institute, Inc. Does it work? Read a letter from Dabney Lessman, whose brother used the program. Dabney, being a teenager, can be trusted not to pull any punches:

Dear Mr. Meyer,

I wish you knew how much CEI has helped my younger brother Darrell. Before he started, my mom dreaded coming home. Every night, Sunday to Thursday, she had to stay up with Darrell until 11 or 12 at night. He might have a simple math problem like 576 + 891, and he would say he didn't know how to do it, and would ask for help, when he did know how to do it. In every single subject he asked for help, when really there was nothing that was too hard for him to do. He came up with some kind of excuse so he didn't have to do it himself. Several times I offered to show him how to figure it out on his own, but he only wanted someone to tell him the answers.

Now Darrell does his homework on his own. He only asks for help on problems he really can't figure out. He's normally in bed by 9:30 or 10. He really enjoys CEI. He told me so. It's amazing how much easier his homework is in four weeks. Just think how it'll be when he gets through! Thank you!!!!! You've made my whole family's life easier. Now my mom can bake cookies while my brother does his homework. She hasn't been able to do this for a long time.

Love in Christ,
Dabney Lessman

Creative Education Institute, Paul believes, is superior even to one-on-one teaching. Even if you have a 1-to-1 teacher ratio, you're still working with a tutorial concept that tries to get something into the child's head without correcting the weaknesses.

The CEI system gives children a degree of control they don't have with an adult teacher, and the program has been met with great success. It is currently being used by hundreds of school systems in Texas, positively affecting thousands of children.

Families perpetuate giving, too

Paul recalls a lesson he was taught by a wealthy European friend. Paul had taken the man aside at a charitable reception and said, "I want to ask you something, Sean. Why do you bother with all this? You've got more money than all these people put together. Why don't you go live happily on one of your Greek islands?"

Paul was being deliberately provocative, and he received a provocative answer. Sean replied, "When I was five years old, my dad took me to the poor section of town and told me, 'But for the grace of God, you and I would be living here. Never forget that God wants to use our lives helping these people and everyone else who needs ministering to.' That made a profound impact on my life."

"That made an impression on me too," says Paul. "And it's what I'm doing with my family now. Every time we minister to somebody, I try to have one of my children or one of my grandchildren there."

Paul says, "I would like to be a role model to my family, my associates, and other business people, to run their lives in a Christ-like fashion and to

> Why should men leave great fortunes to their children? If this is done from affection, is it not misguided affection? Observation teaches that, generally speaking, it is not well for the children that they should be so burdened.
> — Andrew Carnegie

operate their businesses with Christian principles. It is my hope they would dedicate a far greater part of their earnings to stewardship, both from their companies and individually."

LETTER OF THANKS

Mr. and Mrs. Meyer,

Allow me to introduce myself. My name is Strib Stribling. Thanks to you I am the Development Director for Reach Out Youth Solutions, a wonderful ministry in Atlanta, Georgia.

You gave a forward-thinking gift to Reach Out Youth Solutions for the express purpose of hiring a Development Director. Because of the gift you provided, Reach Out was able to thoughtfully, patiently, and prayerfully look for "God's right man" for the job of raising money for the ministry.

I personally owe you a debt of gratitude for both your generosity and stewardship. You planted the seed and started the process of multiplying money and ministry. You are allowing me to do something I love.

Sincerely yours,
Strib Stribling
Reach Out Youth Solutions

Can your giving continue on forever?

What is going to happen to your money, real estate, stocks, and other investments., when you die? Andrew Carnegie more than once expressed the view that wealth should be given away in life, not in death.

In fact, Carnegie said: "I would as soon leave to my son a curse as the almighty dollar." He wasn't talking about giving his money to his children; he was talking about giving his money away to a charity or cause that would help others.

Carnegie himself gave away 90% of his fortune before he died.

Paul intends to leave this world with nothing more to his name than he can fit in a suitcase. The main goal of his businesses is to make money to put into their family foundation.

Carnegie took steps to ensure that the wealth he generated remains protected and available for charitable use … and Paul and Jane have done the same.

Protecting money is serious business. Cornelius Vanderbilt in 1877, and his son later in 1885, left what were then the largest legacies ever recorded in America. But these resources were systematically squandered, and by the fourth and fifth generation, no Vanderbilt was among the 10 wealthiest Americans. In 1923, only three appeared among the 274 U.S. taxpayers with incomes in excess of a million dollars.

> Wealth is acquired by the daily practice of industry and frugality. He who relies upon these means will rarely be found destitute, and he who relies upon any.other will generally become bankrupt.
> — Francis Wayland

Had Vanderbilt's original $100 million in 1877 been kept intact and reinvested in the leading growth sectors of the American economy, its size a century later would be simply beyond comprehension.

By contrast, Andrew Carnegie, who liquidated his $250 million business interests in 1901 to devote himself to selecting and supervising projects of philanthropy, soon found his annual income of $12.5 million too large an amount to administer.

It was Carnegie, therefore, who pioneered the solution of creating a series of perpetual trusts for the support of education, scientific research, international peace, and various other causes.

John D. Rockefeller followed suit. Like Carnegie, he detested high society extravagance, but unlike Carnegie, he had made a habit of tithing as early as the 1850s when he first brought home a wage. He gave away over half his fortune before he died — a fortune whose value peaked at around a billion dollars in 1913.

LETTER OF THANKS

My name is Ricky Edison. I am the Assistant Principal at Bell's Hill Elementary, University Middle, and University High School. While I was in high school, I started attending the Boys Club. There I learned about a program called Passport to Success.

I attended McLennan Community College for two years and then transferred to Baylor University where I earned my Bachelor of Science in Education in 1996. My college education was paid for by you.

I have never had the opportunity to meet you, but I wanted to take this time to tell you thank you. I do not know what I would have done without this help.

Sincerely,
Ricky Edison

In addition to that, Rockefeller established a series of foundations and institutes between 1900 and 1914 to oversee the long-term distribution of his charitable funds. The tycoon's legacy of philanthropy passed from father to son, with John D. Rockefeller, Jr., saying, "I have been brought up to believe that giving ought to be entered into in just the same careful way as investing — that giving is investing, and that it should be tested by the same intelligent standard." In today's dollars, Rockefeller's worth would be over 300 billion dollars, making him the richest man in the past 1,000 years!

The charitable institute/foundation is here to stay. But if you think such things are reserved for the ultra-rich, think again. Almost anyone can establish a foundation — and probably many of us should.

To ensure that your giving continues long after you have died is to tap into the power of replication. Replication empowers others to do what you have done; it teaches others to do what you did; and it shows others how to perform as you would perform with the same or even greater quantity, quality, and attitude.

Now that is giving!

Options to consider

Numerous financial instruments are available to you. I recommend these three for your review:

#1 — Give to a Charitable Gift Annuity

> In brief, a charitable gift annuity allows you to make a gift to your favorite charity and continue to receive an income. The charity, in return for cash or property, agrees to pay a fixed sum of money for a period measured by one or two lives. The person who contributes an asset to the annuity is usually, but not always, the person who receives payments. [See Appendix A for a more complete description.]

#2 — Form a Trust

> In brief, there are many types of trusts, but the one main benefit of all trusts is how they keep your estate out of probate after your death. Trusts are often confused with wills, but the main difference between the two is the fact that with a trust your property will not go through the court system, or probate, when you die. With a will the transfer of property takes place at your death and goes through

probate to determine the legalities of the will and the properties being dispersed. During probate much of the estate is taken by taxes and sometimes attorneys. When you create a trust, you transfer your properties to it while you are still alive and it continues on through your death. [See Appendix B for a more complete description.]

#3 — Create a Private Foundation

In brief, a private foundation is a separate legal entity formed and controlled by a person or a family and qualified to support a wide range of charitable work in accordance with the donor's wishes. Though not a public charity, it qualifies for the same tax-exempt status under the Internal Revenue code, and any donations made to it are deductible as charitable contributions for federal income tax purposes. [See Appendix C for a more complete description.]

If you think any of these options may be right for you, my advice is to contact your CPA or financial advisor and work up a specific plan. That way you are using his or her expertise to make sure that your giving continues forever.

Good job, steward!

"What you are in the sight
of God; that you truly are."

— *Anonymous*

CHAPTER 11

How Will You Be Remembered?

There is old saying that if you want to know how people will talk about you when you are gone, write your own epitaph now and then live that way!

What would your epitaph say? How do you want to be remembered?

Epitaphs are usually one-liners that capture the essence of a person's life. Since there is no rule that prohibits having more than one epitaph, here are 13 epitaphs Paul told me he would choose for himself:

He loved God first.
He loved his family and extended family.
He loved his friends.
He was a giver.
He was an encourager.
He forgave!
He kept his word.
He honored God with his life.
He always had a positive attitude.
He was not ashamed of the gospel of Jesus Christ.
He was a role model.
He contributed to his community.
He consistently helped others.

Although we like great things said about us, it all comes down to the reality of our actions. What we do has a greater effect than anything we say.

You may not get a 2nd chance

When Paul was 12 years old and in the Boy Scouts, his best friend, Billy Farnham and he went camping with 3,000 other scouts in the mountains of California. During the night, Billy lit a candle inside their tent (perhaps he was scared) and then fell asleep. The candle ignited his sleeping bag and he burned to death.

Paul escaped without a scratch. Paul promised Billy's father who was the scoutmaster that he would grow up to be a scout for both of them. But he still wondered, "Why him and not me?"

We don't always get a second chance. As adults, we often miss what is most important in life until it is too late. Many people could easily interchange their name for Joe's in the following story:

> Our true acquisitions lie only in our charities — we gain only as we give.
> — William Gilmore Simms

While he was on his deathbed, Joe's family asked him what he wished he had done while he still could. Instead of listing all the things he had spent years pursuing and dreaming about, such as a bigger house, the ultimate job, more investments, or better vacations. Joe's wish list was short and simple.

He wished he had spent more time with his family, gone to Europe with his wife, attended his kid's ballgames, taken his grandkids out for lunch more often, and not worked as much. **The only reference to work was wishing he had done less of it.**

During life's most trying times, what is most important instantly comes to the surface while the unimportant suddenly becomes inconsequential. Sadly, many come to that revelation too late.

In that vein, Paul relayed the following to me:

> A long time ago I purposed that I would do today what I would wish I had done tomorrow. This perspective allows me to enjoy many special times with other people.

Life is short. Paul wants to make the most of every day because tomorrow is not guaranteed. We must all seize the day.

LETTER OF THANKS

The day has finally come — I am going to graduate from college! I would never have made it this far without the Passport to Success Foundation.

I am the first person in my family to ever graduate from college with a bachelor's degree. I am very proud and feel I have accomplished the goals I had set out to achieve.

Respectfully,
Kera M.

Habits that help you "seize the day"

Paul and Jane are true believers that certain habits will enable us to live life to its fullest, making the most of every opportunity. These habits are not personality traits! They are little choices that we internalize into habits.

Here are 13 of Paul and Jane's favorite habits that can help you seize each day:

1. **Be a giver:** Our greatest joy is giving!

2. **Be positive:** Being positive has the potential of turning the worst situations into victories.

3. **Be thankful:** We always give thanks, keep our eyes on God as our provider, and keep a smile on our face.

4. **Be a quick forgiver:** We don't have time to waste in unforgiveness.

5. **Be optimistic:** Believing the best of people and circumstances is a sure way to find the best.

> A road that perhaps more than any other leads to self atrophy is undedicated money.
> — E. Stanley Jones

6. **Be an inverted paranoid:** We believe the whole world is conspiring to do only good things for us.

7. **Be an encourager:** Encouragers make us feel better, stronger, and more capable of accomplishing our dreams. We want to do the same for others.

8. **Be spontaneous:** We have a sense of urgency and a do-it-now attitude.

9. **Smile a lot and laugh at life:** We laugh more than anyone we know.

10. **Live life with enthusiasm:** We will only live once, so why not give it our all?

11. **Enjoy life:** We truly enjoy life.

12. **Find a hobby you enjoy:** No matter where we are, we have something we like to do.

13. **Look for people to help:** We get up every morning excited about the person we might help that day.

Give now or give later?

No doubt you have heard of the miserly individual who dies and leaves millions of dollars to a college. Is this an example for us to follow?

Consider this:

> "Posthumous charities are the very essence of selfishness when bequeathed by those who, even alive, would part with nothing." — Charles Caleb Colton

There are others who give now, and when they die, their giving comes to an end. Is this an example for us to follow?

> I do not believe one can settle how much we ought to give. I am afraid the only safe rule is to give more than we can spare. There ought to be things we should like to do and cannot do because our charitable expenditures excludes them.
> — C. S. Lewis

Consider this:

> "[When I die] if I leave behind me ten pounds ... you and all mankind [may] bear witness against me, that I have lived and died a thief and a robber." — John Wesley

Give now or give later? That is a question that I believe can be answered with two words: **<u>Do both</u>**.

Consider this:

> "All you have shall some day be given: Therefore give now, that the season of giving may be yours and not your inheritors." — Kahlil Gibran

Why not give now *AND* give in such a way that the giving continues?

Paul and Jane are great examples of this. They are active givers now and they have taken steps to ensure that numerous charities, causes, and ministries will have ongoing support long after they have passed away.

To me, that's having your cake and eating it too! Why not be a blessing and be blessed every step of the way.

After all:

> "The currency of this world will be worthless at our death or at Christ's return, both of which are imminent." — Randy C. Alcorn

Answering life's final questions

Nate Meleen, a long-time friend from Paul's childhood days, once told him, **"My life's goal is that when I die, not one thing God has planned for me will be left unfinished."**

Now that is a great perspective!

Legendary author and speaker, Charlie "Tremendous" Jones, sent Paul a personal note a few weeks before Charlie died at age 80 after a long fight with cancer. Part of the note read:

> God has allowed me to know and be influenced by many great lives. I thank God you are one of them. When I first met you, it was difficult to understand how one so young could be so successful. I don't think you or I realized how wonderfully God had chosen and anointed you. Because I was young in the Lord, I didn't see this until I read *The Art of Giving* (the original version of this book) and I knew immediately you were a very special man that God chose to do great and mighty things through.

Those are powerful words!

When our goal as stewards is to accomplish God's will and hear, *"Well done, good and faithful servant!"* (Matthew 25:21), questions like "What do you wish you had done while you still could?" and "What do you want your epitaph to say?" will answer themselves.

When all is said and done, one final question remains: "How do I want to be remembered?"

Your answer to that question will reveal how you lived, breathed, and died — you lived as a **steward**!

Appendix A

Charitable Gift Annuities

What is a charitable gift annuity? In brief, a charitable gift annuity allows you to make a gift to a charity and continue to receive an income for yourself or for others.

You are signing a contract which states that a charity, in return for the property or cash that you give them, will pay you a set amount of money for a set amount of time. The payments are agreed upon, are contractually binding, and do not fluctuate, regardless of what the stock market or interest rates are doing.

Naturally, the payments are based on how much you give or the value of your gift, as well as the period of time that payments are to be made.

Because the charity uses the gift for the charity's intended purposes, the charitable gift annuity rates will be lower than the rates from other institutions.

Is a charitable gift annuity right for you? Consider a charitable gift annuity …

- If you have stocks that you want to sell but do not want to pay capital gains on.
- If you want a set residual income that will continue as long as you live.
- If your fixed-income investments have declined.
- If the interest rates on your CDs have dropped.
- If you want to pass on a fixed income to a family member, and avoid probate as well.

Not all charities offer charitable gift annuities, so contact your favorite charity and see if they offer gift annuities. Gather all the information they have available, and then meet with your financial planner and your tax accountant. Discuss all the details so that you are well prepared as you make this important decision.

Again, if you are considering a charitable gift annuity, please discuss this with your financial planner.

Appendix B

Creating a Trust

Why should you create a trust? Quite simply: to avoid probate.

Probate is the court system that decides what to do with your estate after you have died. This process is lengthy and costly. But with a trust, you can avoid probate because your estate is transferred to your desired beneficiary while you are still living.

While you are alive, you transfer your estate (money, stocks, real estate, etc.) through your trust to the beneficiary or beneficiaries that you have selected.

Do you still own your estate? No, your trust does, but you continue to have access and control. In essence, it's still yours, just not in your name.

Is creating a trust right for you? Consider a trust …

- If you have assets over $500,000.
- If you want to create a scholarship fund.
- If you want to avoid probate and save taxes.
- If you want to keep certain family members from getting part of your estate.

If you are considering creating a trust, ask your financial planner or tax accountant for referrals. You will need a lawyer with experience in both tax planning and estate planning.

Take your time to do this right.

Appendix C

Forming a Foundation

What is a foundation? A foundation is:

> An entity that is established as a nonprofit corporation or a charitable trust, with a principal purpose of making grants to unrelated organizations or institutions or to individuals for scientific, educational, cultural, religious, or other charitable purposes. (foundationcenter.org)

There are two basic types of foundations: private and public. A private foundation is usually funded from one person, business, or family. A public foundation, on the other hand, gets its funding from the public, which includes many individuals, businesses, and government agencies.

Are you thinking of forming a foundation? Contact your financial planner and your tax accountant. Get their insights and their referrals.

Here are a few details to consider about a foundation:

> The tax laws for private foundations include, among other things, a minimum distribution requirement, an excise tax on investment income, and a limit as to the proportion of a for-profit enterprise they may own, the "excess business holdings" rule. Private foundations must make "qualifying distributions" of at least 5% of the average market value of their investment assets in any given fiscal year by the end of the following year, a rule often referred to as "the payout requirement." The excise tax, normally 2% of net investment income, or 1% in special circumstances, counts as a credit toward the 5% minimum. (foundationcenter.org)

The IRS has certain requirements for all foundations. You will learn these as you consult with your financial planner and tax accountant.

Foundations offer great freedom and opportunities to those who create and manage them effectively.

Appendix D

Resources

Websites for setting up a foundation or charity:

Private Foundation.com
www.theprivatefoundation.com

CHARITYSMITH National Society of Memorial Funds
www.charitysmith.org

Charity Registration.com
www.charity-registration.com

Foundation Center
www.foundationcenter.org

IRS
www.irs.gov

Websites for setting up a trust:

Ehow.com
www.ehow.com

Make a trust (article)
www.nolo.com

Books for setting up a trust:

The Complete Book of Trusts, 3rd Edition (paperback) by Martin M. Shenkman

The Living Trust: The Failproof Way to Pass Along Your Estate to Your Heirs by Henry W. Abts

Books for starting a non-profit foundation or charity:

Starting and Managing a Nonprofit Organization: A legal guide by Bruce R. Hopkins (2009)

The Nonprofit Handbook: Everything you need to know to start by Gary M. Grobman (2008)

How to Form a Nonprofit Corporation by Anthony Mancuso (2007)

Starting & Building a Nonprofit: A practical guide by Peri H. Pakroo (2007)

About the Author

Dr. William M. "Bill" Hinson is a graduate of Baylor University in Waco, Texas. He earned a Master of Divinity degree from Southwestern Baptist Theological Seminary and the Doctor of Ministry degree from the New Orleans Baptist Theological Seminary. Bill has pastored churches in Miami and Fort Lauderdale, Florida, and New Orleans, Louisiana.

Dr. Hinson's speaking engagements include preaching to 160,000 in India, preaching the annual sermon of the Southern Baptist Convention with over 16,000 in attendance, and speaking at the U.S. Military Academy at West Point, New York, as well as the Rose Garden at the White House. He represented President Gerald Ford as an ambassador-at-large at the XII Winter Olympic Games at Innsbruck, Austria. Over the years, he has made 45 trips around the world.

His awards and recognitions include the 1981 George Washington Medal of Honor from Freedoms Foundation at Valley Forge for his patriotic sermons and writings. The *Saturday Evening Post* featured him in an article called "The American Minister." An endowed chair in Christian Scriptures at Truett Theological Seminary at Baylor University bears Dr. Hinson's name. He was also honored with the George W. Truett Distinguished Church Service Award at Baylor University.

From 1989 until his election as president of Haggai Institute in 1995, Bill Hinson represented Haggai Institute as vice president for international liaisons. During that same period, he served as executive assistant to Paul J. Meyer, founder of Success Motivation Institute in Waco, Texas. Before that, Dr. Hinson spent nearly four years as special assistant to the president of Baylor University.

Dr. Hinson became CEO and Vice-Chairman of Haggai Institute in 2001. Bill and his wife, Bettye, have two children and six grandchildren.

If you want to know more about
Paul J. Meyer and his many
books, CDs, DVDs, and booklets,
simply go to:
www.pauljmeyer.com.

I know you will be encouraged
and challenged by any and all
Paul J. Meyer products.

Enjoy!

Dr. William. M. "Bill" Hinson